Real Estate
Influence

By Chris Stuart
With Allan Dalton

Foreword by Charlie Oppler, NAR® President
Introduction by Neal Schaffer, Author

D0067411

The authors of **Real Estate Influence** have and
will not receive any remuneration from the sale
of this book. All profits from this book will be
donated to *The Sunshine Kids Foundation*—
save for printing, publishing, and administration
costs. *The Sunshine Kids Foundation* is a
not-for-profit that adds quality of life to children
with cancer by providing them with exciting, positive group activities, so they may once again do
what kids are meant to do—have fun and celebrate
life! Learn more at SunshineKids.org

This book has no affiliation with HSF Affiliates LLC,
Berkshire Hathaway HomeServices or Real Living—
and solely represents the individual views and opinions of Chris Stuart and Allan Dalton.

ISBN 9798710219713

Printed in the United States of America.

For Want of a Nail

For the want of a nail the shoe was lost,
For the want of a shoe the horse was lost,
For the want of a horse the rider was lost,
For the want of a rider the battle was lost,
For the want of a battle the kingdom was lost,
And all for the want of a horseshoe-nail.

— Centuries-old, unattributed Proverb

For Want of Real Estate Influence

For want of influence,
Respect was lost
For want of respect,
Credibility was lost
For want of credibility,
Value was lost
For want or value,
Income was lost
For want of income,
Careers were lost
For want of careers,
An industry was lost
All for the want of influence.

— Chris Stuart / Allan Dalton

Dedications

To my wife, Monica, and our children,
Gabriella, Austin, and Juliana

To my mentor, Gino Blefari

The Key to Successful Leadership Today
is Influence, Not Authority.
— Ken Blanchard

Acknowledgement

Allan and I want to acknowledge the invaluable contributions of Thomas Ryan Ward (aka Ryan The Designer) in the production of this book—and for making himself available at our convenience as we devoted countless weekends throughout the year writing Real Estate Influence.

Real Estate *Influence Chapters*

LINKS

"In Real Estate Influence, Chris Stuart and Allan Dalton bring a unique wealth of real world knowledge and experience to share that will positively impact and transform your business forever."
— **Dermot Buffini**, CEO, Buffini & Company

Foreword by Charlie Oppler

Real Estate Influence means different things to different people. How often did we hear, as children, our parents implore us that we should not play or hang out with certain people because they were a bad influence?

Perhaps not as frequently did we also hear who might represent a good influence. The National Association of REALTORS® exists so that REALTORS® can favorably influence consumers and communities, and in a professionally positive fashion. I agreed to accept the honor of writing the foreword to Chris Stuart's book on influence for reasons of influence.

I seek any credible industry platform to speak out and influence others regarding the importance of diversity, inclusivity, and Fair Housing. Such strong beliefs and commitments are equally important to Chris Stuart.

Moreover, as a long-standing former agent and for many years now a broker-owner, I completely respect the distinctions which Chris Stuart and Allan Dalton persuasively assert in *Real Estate Influence* between real estate image and real estate influence.

It pleases me that a source of inspiration for Chris' guidance on how to close what he refers to as the Real Estate Loyalty Gap came from research provided by the National Association of REALTORS® annual report.

I would like to thank every reader of this book who is a member of the National Association of REALTORS® as well as real estate professionals throughout the world for the millions of individuals and families whom they serve annually through their service, skills, and yes— ever-evolving influence.

Charlie Oppler
President, National Association of REALTORS®

Introduction by Neal Schaffer

When I wrote *The Age of Influence*, a book explaining the power of digital influence and how businesses should redefine their social media presence, I envisioned that its principles could be applied by marketing teams and entrepreneurs in any industry. What I didn't realize was how it might revitalize industries that needed to reinvent themselves.

What you are about to read is how Chris Stuart, the CEO of Berkshire Hathaway HomeServices, together with former CEO of Realtor.com and current CEO of Real Living Real Estate, Allan Dalton, are on a mission to reimagine the real estate professional's role in his or her community in the age of influence.

As you begin to read this book, you will realize just as I did that the real estate industry needs real estate influence to remain a relevant, value-add industry in the Internet era. Fortunately, *Real Estate Influence* unlocks the mindset that industry leaders need to understand to avoid becoming a forgotten entity in the near future.

Real Estate Influence makes the case that a revolution is needed for the real estate industry to survive. Fortunately, Chris Stuart has emerged as the leader in helping the real estate industry discover and leverage the full and yet to be realized influence of its community.

Why aren't consumers loyal to their real estate agents? The answer, Chris Stuart asserts, is in their lack of influence. *Real Estate Influence* provides a blueprint for both industry leaders and day-to-day practitioners to begin the process of teaching their network the why and how of leveraging influence to foster broader, deeper, and greater revenue-generating influence.

While my book, *The Age of Influence*, was written primarily for businesses to help them tap into and expand their digital influence, *Real Estate Influence* focuses on the unique challenges the internet-driven economy presents for all real estate professionals. Real estate professionals, unlike corporate social media and marketing executives, derive their influence primarily through and within their community. As I read this ground-breaking book, I realized that real estate professionals are a unique hybrid of salespeople and marketers, each individual being a small business owner of their own company. When they can begin to translate the evergreen business and networking concepts of like, know, and trust to the digital world through the lens of *Real Estate Influence*, they will begin to realize their potential as a value-add professional, gaining respect for what they do in a similar way to other respected professions.

One thing is certain: *Real Estate Influence* shows that the real estate industry benefits in having Chris Stuart as a leader in a long overdue crusade to elevate real estate influence.

Neal Schaffer
Author of *The Age of Influence*

Chapter 1—
"My Why"

As CEO of Berkshire Hathaway HomeServices, I am forever mindful that the future success of real estate organizations, teams, and individual real estate professionals, will depend upon the degree in which conventional methods of consumer engagement and influence are transformed.

While no one person, brand, or brokerage alone will serve as the solitary catalyst for such required changes, my purpose for writing this book is, at the very least, to make a meaningful contribution to the dialogue and decisions regarding how real estate influence can be optimized with consumers, clients, and communities. Change from within, I must acknowledge, can be painstakingly slow—reminding me of the following quote:

"The conventional view serves to protect us from the painful job of thinking."

These are the evocative words of John Kenneth Galbraith, legendary and controversial Canadian/American economist.

Dr. Galbraith, a former Harvard University professor, was an iconic scholar who is responsible for the book titled *The Age of Uncertainty*. The term "conventional wisdom" is credited to Galbraith. I purposely selected his quote to begin *Real Estate Influence,* as the ongoing role and value of real estate professionals will require a departure from "conventional wisdom." While the real estate industry is not collectively guilty of any consensus as erroneous as that of our ancestors, who believed the world to be flat, many of the real estate industry's conventional views, in my opinion, require reconsideration.

A significant degree of modern-day real estate groupthink, or "conventional wisdom," may very well be undermining or impeding change related to the elevation of perceived real estate professional value. There are innumerable examples of when real estate conventional wisdom of the past stultified progress and left the real estate industry vulnerable to external and opposing influences. To a monolithic degree, the real estate industry first resisted the internet. This resistance was ill-advised. Years later, the real estate industry naively battled IDX. This was wrong. Twentyfive years ago, the conventional wisdom was that the real estate industry would be disintermediated—as was the travel industry. This prediction was also erroneous. When the threat of disintermediation subsided, its dissipation came with an alternative warning. Specifically that the industry would now encounter another dreaded D-word: complete disruption. Such conventional wisdom was also wrong.

Regarding complete real estate disruption, I have not attended a conference any time during the past fifteen years where the looming threat of disruption was not the centerpiece of concern. Oftentimes, "conventional wisdom" is wrong and, obviously, not just within real estate. For example, consuming a big and healthy breakfast of eggs, bacon, buttered toast, and grits was the conventional wisdom when I was growing up in Texas. Later, this large and hearty breakfast was presumed unhealthy. Today for many, it has once more become a recommended way to start the day. At one point, "conventional wisdom" informed that coffee causes cancer, and next, we are led to believe coffee is preventative.

The purpose of this book is not only to challenge current conventional real estate wisdom but, more importantly, to examine overlooked opportunities. A major opportunity, which I believe must be seized, is to more effectively, efficiently, and positively engage and influence real estate consumers. Most importantly, influence must extend well beyond the real estate transactional role. External forces are increasingly mounting in well-funded attempts to marginalize the perceived value of real estate agents. These initiatives mandate a need to make these current and future times the "Age of Real Estate Influence."

Before I address additional reasons why we must introduce an "Age of Real Estate Influence," along with prescribed changes, please indulge me in two personal observations. Another reason why I began this book by referencing John Kenneth Galbraith is that Dr. Galbraith began his academic career as a bio-science major at Ontario Agricultural College. He went on to receive Master of Science and Doctor of Philosophy degrees in Agriculture Economics at the University of California at Berkeley. Similarly, I majored in bio-science at an agricultural university, Texas A&M. I am now responsible for the economics of two real estate brands (while not the brokerages themselves). I point out my science and agricultural similarity with Dr. Galbraith humbly, as long before he went on to become President of the American Economic Association, he was clearly and profoundly influenced by the relationship between the ecosystems found in biology and economics. Moreover, their relationship to man-made societal, business, and economic order shaped his teaching. The nexus between physical nature and human nature is my passion, as well. It is a relationship that guides and informs me to a considerable degree. Unquestionably, my perspective directed towards successful real estate-related systems was formed long before my years at Oracle and my many years in the real estate industry. Accordingly, you can anticipate that part of my proposed solutions for the challenges the real estate industry will increasingly encounter arise from this foundation.

My second personal observation has to do with my philosophical approach to writing this book. My willingness to share my thoughts, along with Allan Dalton's, with the real estate industry at large—rather than limiting this content to the brands and networks I serve—also emanates from the very nature of ecosystems. The real estate industry undeniably operates as its own unique ecosystem. The real estate industry's ecosystem consists of a pronounced level of symbiotic sharing. The entire sharing of property information evolved from the spirit and rules governing cooperation. Realtor.com, MLS, IDX, and, above all, the National Association of Realtors® are both tributes and tributaries for the symbiotic and synergistic sharing of information and knowledge. This real estate ecosystem operates opposite to the parasitic and selfish exploitation of business opportunities found elsewhere. Such cooperation however must always, first and foremost, benefit consumers and clients, as well as the real estate industry. This ethos also requires the complete support of diversity, inclusion, and Fair Housing laws.

The real estate industry must fully understand that there are both pluses and minuses that can result through high-level organization and industry unity. A positive aspect of industry unity is an immense symbiosis regarding education and idea-sharing. This phenomenon is also reflected in my reasons for writing this book. Who amongst us has not attended a NAR Convention and listened while a speaker or coach presented ideas to an audience consisting of competing organizations? This industry-wide ecosystem, and specifically its symbiosis, is the unique connective tissue that professionally amalgamates and empowers the real estate industry. Sharing, for me as a CEO, means offering my perspective on industry challenges and solutions. I must acknowledge, however, that I do so without revealing my brand-specific systems and solutions. These differentiated programs I reserve expressly for my networks. However, regarding that which I can and will share, I believe that if most of the industry does not work together to make the next few decades and beyond the "Age of Real Estate Influence," that no one company or brand alone, will succeed in changing consumer perceptions in the ways necessary.

Individual insurance company transformation and outcomes would have been significantly limited had insurance companies, like John Hancock or Metropolitan Life, alone made the unilateral decision to establish a difference between the way consumers perceive the role of a life insurance agent versus the expanded value of a financial planner. To that point, I encourage all other industry leaders to assist and empower your brokers and network associates to optimize their real estate-related value and influence by including that which makes your brand and brokerage distinct.

For example, I am working aggressively (along with my teams) to achieve this objective through the development and introduction of what I have branded the The Real Estate IQ System. This system is designed to increase and measure individual and brokerage influence quotients as a precursor to measuring market share. I will outline in this book the many areas which require both greater horizontal and vertical influence to elevate the perceived value of what real estate agents in general represent. Such sharing comes with the acknowledgment that the only way we can truly create an "Age of Real Estate Influence" is for the real estate profession, in general, to become more influential to all real estate consumers. Now that I have provided some of my personal "whys" for creating this book, I will now identify the larger "why" behind making this the "Age of Real Estate Influence."

I strategically spoke to this very subject during a recent convention speech. That's when I offered that the greatest definition I've heard as to why disruption takes place is, "When something no longer makes sense." Blockbuster no longer made sense. Hello Netflix! Travel agents no longer made sense due to Expedia, and many malls no longer make sense. Amazon does. Simply put, these disruptors influenced consumers in a way that made more significant sense than their purged predecessors.

Now let's consider the threat of real estate disruption. As mentioned earlier, the first level of conventional wisdom, years ago, was that there existed a serious threat surrounding the most profound case of disruption, that being real estate disintermediation. Thankfully, disintermediation, which means the elimination of the middle person, never occurred. Who is the middle person? You, the real estate professional. Conventional wisdom, here again, was wrong. The thinking back then was homeowners would find a way, as they did with eBay, to post their home as a product directly to buyers. This consumer-direct auction, mega for-sale-by-owner (FISBO), or bidding site would eliminate the need to go through a real estate agent. All that would be required would be to merely assemble the mortgage, appraisal, escrow, legal functions, and services, which would also be conveniently advertised on these sites. This prognosticated disintermediation never occurred. Nor do I believe it ever will. My optimism is due to the immense complexities and the protracted nature of a real estate negotiated contract and the overall indispensable skills of a real estate agent. Skills such as negotiation, staging, and keeping transactions favorably moving forward amidst innumerable potential deal killers, will always preempt any threats regarding potential disintermediation.

Instead of disintermediation or outright disruption, the real estate industry has only experienced partial disruption. This limited disruption also only emerged on the buying side of the transaction. Partial buying-side disruption resulted due to how over 95% of buyers begin their search on the internet. Partial buying-side disruption, however, only delays the involvement of a real estate agent. The real estate industry can give a sigh of relief that this limited degree of disruption has not led to the elimination of the buyer-agent. Disruption surrounding how buyers now first begin their search, without the need for an agent, was not economically harmful. To the contrary, if a homeseller were to begin the marketing of their property before engaging the services of a real estate agent, then that would be catastrophically harmful. I believe listing-side partial disruption could be significantly injurious to both consumers and real estate professionals. Unlike the threat of listing-side disruption, a case can be made that the value of many real estate agents has actually been elevated due to buying-side partial disruption. Preventing or minimizing partial listing-side disruption will involve the real estate profession becoming more pre-eminent, prestigious, and influential—characteristics emanating from superior knowledge, trusted advice, and influence. This aspirational evolution will require a significant change in the ways in which consumers perceive the role and influence of real estate professionals in general.

I remember from my first days at Oracle how I instantly, as did everyone else in the company, benefit from the respect afforded both Larry Ellison and Oracle. As many of you have probably read or heard, in the Information Age, data and information represent lower levels of value than knowledge and wisdom. Now that consumers enjoy unlimited access to home and lifestyle-related data and information, the knowledge and wisdom of real estate agents required to refine, distill and contextualize information and housing data, in order for consumers to arrive at prudent decisions, has become significantly more valuable. Attaining this knowledge and wisdom-based value will also exponentially increase influence and prestige.

In the "Age of Real Estate Influence," while the real estate industry will still be the source for select data and information, it must be acknowledged that consumers can access much of this information on their own. Therefore, to optimize influence, the real estate industry will have to exponentially increase the dissemination of its indispensable knowledge and wisdom. This elevated role would not be the case if we could simply freeze the way in which most real estate consumers now use the internet; that is predominantly as a tool to search for homes and not agents. If the internet were to remain the exclusive incentive for consumers to merely search for properties and not real estate professionals, I would not be writing this book.

This singular reason for real estate search, which has led to partial buying-side disruption, fortunately, has not led to a compensatory related challenge to real estate agent value. The same economic outcome, however, will not be the case should the internet lead to an equivalent and partial disruption regarding the listing-side. While partial buying-side disruption did not lead to perceived value erosion, listing-side partial disruption unquestionably will; for the following reasons:

"Listing-side disruption" will find home sellers enticed through well-subsidized off and online advertisements seeking to seduce sellers based on well-publicized proclaimed discounts, ratings, reviews, and rebates. Such ubiquitous and timely promotion will provide links to websites expressly devoted to educating home sellers on how to select their real estate agent more intelligently.

Should homesellers begin to favor the internet when searching for a listing agent (with the same ritualistic devotion they now search for homes), this new environment will call for a different approach—an approach that will elevate influence with homesellers. Specifically, this shift must reflect a depth of influence that exceeds the "industry's conventional wisdom" surrounding the efficacy of traditional prospecting, farming, and social media methods.

Understanding the limitations of conventional thinking, in terms of recognizing the difference between 'disintermediation and disruption,' 'disruption and partial disruption,' 'disruption and devaluation or diminution,' or grasping the imminent listing-side threats will not be either preemptive or preventative for all those determined to protect real and perceived professional real estate value. Knowledge does not automatically lead to a 'game plan' or a 'countervailing response.' In the following chapters, I will examine additional consequences surrounding the insidious role of external forces regarding perceived real estate agent value. I will also provide numerous suggestions and recommendations. My advice hopefully will contribute both to the better understanding of the role of 'off and online real estate-related influence' and how elevated influence, along with real and perceived value amongst consumers, will be required for individual real estate professionals who are resolved to flourish in the future.

I would also like to suggest some additional reasons as to why 'my why' might be 'your why.' Hopefully, you agree with me regarding the need to address and elevate how the media and public both perceive the value of real estate professional influence. Let's begin with the media. Why do you think that anytime the media comments on why real estate values drop, or assesses blame for when there is a real estate related financial crisis, that no fingers are pointed towards the real estate industry? This, counterintuitively, should be a cause for concern. It is generally assumed, among the media, that the real estate industry essentially plays no role in influencing markets regarding whether or when consumers buy and sell real estate. When home sales increased during Covid 19, the media made no connection between the extremely impressive adaptability of real estate professionals to convert their pre-pandemic operations to a virtual platform. It was also highly significant, in 2008, that the real estate industry was never accused of contributing to the epic and worldwide financial collapse. First, I shall cite those who were the identified culprits. That would be every other non-real estate professional stakeholder included in any and all dubious real estate transactions—such as Freddie Mac, Fannie Mae, lenders, credit rating bureaus, and politicians all of whom were lambasted for this real estate related global financial crisis.

Unscathed from all media outcry over this transcendent crisis was the entire real estate industry. Brands, brokerages, real estate professionals, educators, and coaches all were excused from the blame game. While the real estate industry can be pleased not to be found guilty of influencing buyers who bought homes they could not afford, it does raise an evocative question. Why would real estate professionals not be included in the blame when buyers are sold properties they could not afford? The simple answer is that real estate professionals are not responsible for the approval or acquisition of real estate financing and, therefore, it is not their purview to interfere with that aspect of the real estate transactional process.

Yet another level of assessment for why the real estate industry was not factored in the dissection of this epic disaster might be due to its perceived feckless influence. For example, content that announces, "When you are ready to buy or sell a home, give me a call," signals that all decision-making responsibilities remain solely the domain of the consumer and other professionals except real estate professionals (see exhibit).

Whom would you more likely trust regarding advice on whether or not you should invest in real estate?

37.6%	Financial Planner
17.2%	Family, Friends or Neighbors
14.3%	Real Estate Agent
7.0%	Attorney
3.0%	Other
20.9%	None of These

Essentially, by advertising to consumers a message (when read between the lines) that suggests, "When you are ready, then and only then, will I be ready"—a favorite tactic among many real estate professionals— it overtly suggests that real estate decisions should be entirely left to consumers, financial planners, their family and friends. Conversely, if there existed a relationship between real estate professionals and consumers more similar to that of a family doctor, financial planner, or other careers carrying greater prestige and relational trust, then it would be more likely that consumers would reach out to real estate professionals before they made a decision to pursue a specific real estate transaction.

It is difficult to make a case that the real estate industry enjoys enviable influence with consumers or respect, in light of a disturbing Harris Poll. That survey (illustrated in Chapter 11) ranked occupations in terms of prestige. Regrettably, real estate brokers sat at the very bottom of a list of 23 professions (firefighters and doctors were at the top). These findings reveal and reflect how a discernible lack of value, trust, and influence regarding how consumers view the real estate industry and, from my perspective, contribute to the real estate loyalty gap.

The other survey I am presenting is one I personally conducted. This particular research was very responsible for inspiring me to create the IQ system and then, along with Allan Dalton, to write the book *Real Estate Influence.* This research laid the foundation for many of the solutions I present throughout the book. While I will leave it to you to carefully interpret which parts of the survey you find most relevant, I am going to call attention to the two responses I consider the most important and optimistic. Those respondents indicated that they would like to increase their influence and that they are committed to improving their influence.

The inventor and former head of research for General Motors, Charles Kettering, once claimed that "...a problem well stated is half solved." Before reading further, I would like to have everyone who shares my interest in elevating the influence of real estate professionals to be aware of what I believe are the three greatest problems that confront the real estate industry. I do not list the three problems, challenges, and therefore, opportunities in the hope that these issues will suddenly become half-solved but rather as a window into the remainder of the book.

These problems are:

1. The real estate loyalty gap,

2. The inadequate number of sustainable real estate ecosystems,

and

3. The inability of most real estate teams and individual agents to build equity in their business; leading to a lucrative exit strategy.

I began this chapter by referencing how conventional views serve to protect us from the painful job of thinking. The survey I conducted has me convinced that many of real estate's finest professionals are ready to rethink how to increase their relevance, value, and professional influence.

Conventional Wisdom and Its Resistance to Change

Change:	Responses to Change:	
	Industry's 'Initial' (many, but not all) Response	Consumers' Response
Internet	No	Yes
Agency Changes	No	Yes
Enhanced Listings	No	Yes
IDX	No	Yes
Seller Disclosure	No	Yes
Social Networking	Yes, Yes, Yes	Yes

Report for I.Q. System Network Survey

Response Counts

Completion Rate:	78.5%	
Complete		1,551
Partial		424

Totals: 1,975

1. How important is having the ability to influence others in your real estate career?

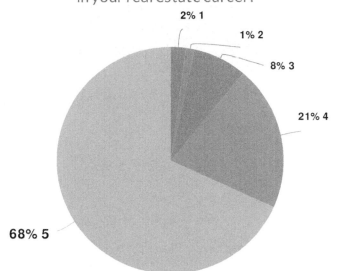

2% 1
1% 2
8% 3
21% 4
68% 5

Value		Percent	Responses
1		2.2%	42
2		1.2%	23
3		7.7%	149
4		20.7%	400
5		68.2%	1,316

Totals: 1,930

2. Where do you believe it is more important to have influence?

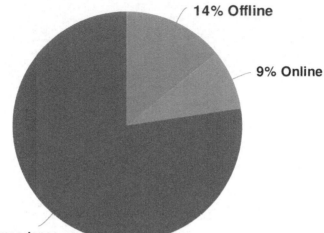

14% Offline

9% Online

77% Equal Importance

Value		Percent	Responses
Offline		14.1%	273
Online		8.5%	164
Equal Importance		77.4%	1,494

Totals: 1,931

3. How would you rank your level of activity within the following?

Item	Overall Rank	Rank Distribution	Score	No. of Rankings
FSBO's	1		9,177	1,638
Door Knocking	2		8,555	1,423
Phone-based prospecting	3		8,105	1,527
Purchased Leads	4		7,971	1,492
Direct Mail	5		7,026	1,607
Geographical Farming	6		6,528	1,524
Open Houses	7		6,285	1,561
Sphere of Influence/Past Clients/Referrals	8		4,678	1,745

Lowest Rank   Highest Rank

17

4. Which of the following would you like to increase your influence and activity?

	Yes	No	Responses
Sphere of Influence/Past Clients/Referrals			
Count	1,732	42	1,774
Row %	97.6%	2.4%	
Open Houses			
Count	1,087	568	1,655
Row %	65.7%	34.3%	
Geographical Farming			
Count	1,406	315	1,721
Row %	81.7%	18.3%	
Direct Mail			
Count	1,255	414	1,669
Row %	75.2%	24.8%	
Door Knocking			
Count	290	1,284	1,574
Row %	18.4%	81.6%	
Purchased Leads			
Count	542	1,052	1,594
Row %	34.0%	66.0%	
Phone-based prospecting			
Count	617	992	1,609
Row %	38.3%	61.7%	
FSBO's			
Count	918	703	1,621
Row %	56.6%	43.4%	
Totals			
Total Responses			1774

5. For your current offline marketing efforts, which of the following tactics are you using?

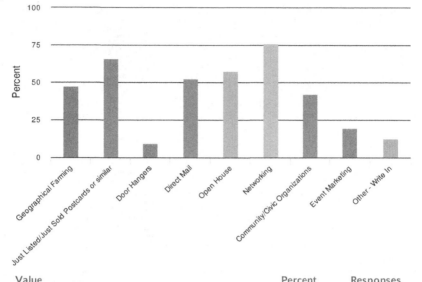

Value		Percent	Responses
Geographical Farming		47.1%	850
Just Listed/Just Sold Postcards or similar		65.7%	1,184
Door Hangers		9.2%	165
Direct Mail		52.3%	943
Open House		57.2%	1,032
Networking		75.9%	1,369
Community/Civic Organizations		42.0%	758
Event Marketing		19.5%	351
Other - Write In		12.3%	222

Other - Write In	Count
Social Media	14
Totals	215

Chapter 2—
Influence and
Your Real Estate Ecosystem

Any CEO of a major real estate brand possesses a sacred responsibility to determine and develop—to the degree possible—systems, services, and solutions by which their brokers, agents, real estate teams, and, ultimately, their brand and network further flourish. Beyond such organizational systems, however, there is also the implicit requirement that CEOs serve as visionaries and thought-leaders. This lofty and anticipated role and function is presumably so she or he will stimulate and optimize superior strategic thinking amongst their respective company(s).

I have spent the past several years, as a part of my leadership responsibilities, devoted to conducting research on how to accomplish this executive imperative. The research and experiential path that has contributed to my thought process regarding real estate-related influence began long before my present position. My years as a bioscience major at Texas A&M, my years as an account executive with Oracle, my tenure as an executive who contributed to the epic success of Intero Real Estate, and the last several years in which I simultaneously serve as the CEO of Berkshire Hathaway HomeServices, Vice Chairman of Real Living, and Executive VP of HomeServices of America, have together shaped the rigorously considered and shared observations presented herein. My thought leadership has indeed been significantly influenced by this background.

Perhaps the greatest and most predictable example of the combined influence drawn from my diverse background can be found in my identifying the importance and need for real estate professionals to create Real Estate Ecosystems. My Real Estate Ecosystem concept evolved from my combined study of ecosystems as a bio-scientist, my experience with systematic solutions from my years at Oracle, and the challenges I have learned that real estate professionals typically encounter and will increasingly face moving forward.

How would you define an ecosystem? We all have a general sense of its meaning, but it is always helpful to employ a precise definition in order to enjoy a completely clear understanding of the term. An ecosystem is a community of organisms interrelated with their physical environment. There are four major ecosystems: Terrestrial, Lentic, Lotic, and Artificial. Terrestrial refers to an ecosystem that is comprised of forests, deserts, grasslands, tundra, and coastal areas. Lentic refers to aquatic with land combination, such as ponds, rivers, lakes, swamps, and streams. Lotic ecosystems, as I remember one of my favorite professors enunciating LO-TIC, is made up of bodies of both fresh and salt waters that run to the sea or ocean. During my years as a resident of Sacramento (my family and I now live in Lake Tahoe), I was constantly reminded of my love for ecosystems and, in this case, Lotic ecosystems. Specifically, when I observed the Sacramento River and how it flows into the San Joaquin River, then into the San Francisco Bay, under the Golden Gate Bridge, and finally merging into the mighty Pacific. The Sacramento River, being a part of a larger ecosystem, enjoys a symbiosis and significance that goes well beyond the environs of California's state capital.

The fourth ecosystem is an artificial ecosystem, which is no stranger to bio-scientists that also study artificial ecosystems. As the name suggests, these are systems that are so-called man-made. Canals and reservoirs being prime examples, along with bio-modes created by bio-scientists for research purposes.

Since this book is devoted to the edification of real estate professionals and not bio-scientists, let's move into a complete real estate realm. Based upon what I have learned from years in real estate, there clearly is a need for real estate professionals to construct a fifth ecosystem. That would be, again, what I am calling a REAL ESTATE ECOSYSTEM.

Let's examine "the why." Anyone who has heard me speak, watched my videos, or participated in my Forever Agent panels, has undoubtedly heard me in foreboding terms, speak of the potential threat—the increased erosion of perceived real estate value. Before I elaborate, let me announce and remind my readers that for both legal, ethical, and matters of cultural ethos, that all real estate fees are negotiable. As you know, there is no set industry fee structure. If that were the case, at least within America, that would be illegal. What I can speak to without any fear of impropriety is that I believe the value which consumers perceive and place upon the service real estate agents provide will be challenged to a greater degree moving forward. I frequently speak of the potential erosion of perceived real estate agent value in general. Disruption, to me, is not a threat (as I mentioned earlier in the book). The greater cause for concern is the diminution of perceived real estate value. Countervailing this threat will require a significant change in how consumers perceive real estate value.

A major way to preemptively inoculate real estate professionals from the possible and insidious threat of diminution of perceived value is through the development of sustainable real estate ecosystems.

What is a Real Estate Ecosystem?

Simply replace the "biological element" of the previously mentioned definition with "humans", and in this case, consumers, clients, vendors, other real estate professionals, and essentially the circle of life that exists within your communities. Thus, a Real Estate Ecosystem is a community of interrelated organisms and their physical environments. All of which you need to influence. Your real estate ecosystem is no different than the symbiosis that occurs within biological ecosystems.

There is, however, one major distinction between biological ecosystems and human ecosystems. Nature, although unpredictable at times, is more sustainably organized than most human approaches to the development of ecosystems. A real estate career begins with a new agent being asked to first document their present sphere of influence. Ironically, this new agent is then encouraged, for the remainder of their career, to acquire and influence strangers versus building upon their current sphere of influence. Allan Dalton, the former CEO of Realtor.com and present-day colleague, says it best, "Sphere of influence is not as important as influencing your sphere."

I have consistently learned that no two agents will ever approach selling, prospecting, presentations, marketing, social networking, etc., in precisely the same way. The same can be said when it comes to the development of one's personal real estate ecosystem. That said, there are, unquestionably, some universal activities that are essential towards that end. Let us begin with how someone new to the real estate industry can begin to develop their real estate ecosystem.

I advise that you let every person you have ever known understand that you are not only in the real estate business, but that you also can assist them in the most likely category of real estate in which they might have an interest. Therefore, do not just announce that you are now in real estate because many consumers do not wish to volunteer to be the real estate equivalent of a medical cadaver—not to mention desiring to help you gain experience at their expense. Also, in the early-on development of your real estate ecosystem, never promote that you just graduated from a so-called fast start or basic training program. Imagine being on an airplane and the pilot announces that this was her or his first flight or that she or he just completed a quick start pilot training program. Such ill-advised statements would serve more as warnings, not announcements. Such a warning or delay of credibility would impede the early development of your real estate ecosystem. Instead, I suggest that you let people within your sphere of influence and developing data/client-base know that you specialize in their area of interest. Think about it. If you point out a special expertise most pertinent to that specific consumer, it is safe to assume that the consumer will automatically infer that you must be in real estate. For example, I advise that the best way for you to announce to senior citizens that you are in the real estate industry is by announcing the benefits of your company's or team's senior lifestyle division.

Additional Tips on
Creating Your Real Estate Ecosystem

The following information is relevant for how to influence consumers, for both newer agents and those most experienced, regarding the development of your real estate ecosystem.

When you meet, phone, post, email, or use a program like Adwerx or Chalk Digital for engagement in a luxury housing segment, your message needs to be, as an example: "Hi John, I wanted you to know that I am part of (your company) Berkshire Hathaway's HomeServices Luxury Division (or Real Living's Luxury Lifestyle Division), and my professional focus is not on just selling more homes, but rather on marketing homes like yours for more." Or, "I just wanted you to know that I am specializing in helping renters to become first time buyers," or, "I am representing many clients in the area that are looking to move to smaller homes to reduce costs and simplify maintenance"—all depending upon the contextual consumer circumstances. Just think about how different that message is than how Jane Doe just joined the company.

2. Your real estate ecosystem development also means sending out to everyone in your sphere of influence a card or a survey that asks, "How can I help you the most this year?"

Converting Vendors and Merchants
into Your Real Estate Ecosystem Network

Here is a potential list that reflects service, services, and skills:

1. Renovating

2. Adding an addition

3. Painting

4. Remodeling

5. Selling your home

6. Buying a home

7. Downsizing (Rightsizing)

8. Moving up

9. Moving with children

10. Moving with pets

11. Investment property

12. Appealing your property taxes

13. Staging

14. Refinancing

15. Real estate strategic planning

16. Landscaping

17. Furniture

18. Pool construction or maintenance

19. Other

Also, create a list of your real estate ecosystem members:

1. Attorney
2. Financial planner
3. Insurance agent
4. Wedding planner
5. Event planner
6. Corporate Re-Lo directors
7. Local florist
8. Doorman or gatekeeper
9. Local store owners
10. CPA
11. Trust officer
12. Divorce attorney
13. Appraiser
14. Landscaper
15. Personal trainer or gym owner
16. Home theatre and entertainment systems
17. Security system installers
18. Home remodelers
19. Interior decorators
20. Civic leaders
21. Local political leaders
22. Leaders of non-profit organizations
23. Leaders within places of worship
24. Fundraisers
25. Environmental groups
26. Real estate podcast host
27. Local real estate media
28. Historical society
29. Plumber, electrician, painter, heating and air conditioning
30. Pet groomers
31. Chamber of commerce
32. Your company's licensed referral network of non-active agents
33. Builders/developers
34. etc.

Creating a real estate ecosystem membership list is the easiest thing you can do. Customizing and adding to your list is something I will leave to you. Your challenge, and thus greatest opportunity, is creating a reciprocal strategy that first establishes a relationship with those with whom you can have an individual relationship. Remember, reciprocity is one of the major elements of creating influence. For example, on the list is pet groomers. Allan Dalton has written a brochure for our networks, Moving with Pets. This enables our agents to visit pet stores and indicate that they would like to send referrals to all of their clients with pets to this business in exchange for having their brochures made available to pet-loving customers.

Moreover, if you created a simple little brochure, you could accomplish in two days of reasonable research and effort on how to sell your home through a divorce, mail it to the divorce attorneys referenced above, and you might receive referrals in return—or you could select a very prominent divorce attorney, and either reference them in your brochure or have them co-author this marketing piece. I'm not going to go through each above-listed ecosystem member one-by-one because that's why you were born with your creative gene. Additionally, I encourage each reader of this book to come up with ways in which to synergistically influence your entire real estate ecosystem. Whether that be showcasing art gallery paintings at your open houses, partnering with a furniture store for staging, hosting home improvement nights or home decorating trends, or having many of these vendors pay for advertising on your personal website. One of the keys is that you want to influence the most influential people off and online. Since there are many real estate professionals who might also be in real estate on your social networking platforms, research which friends and followers have the greatest number of friends and followers and develop relationships and professional networking groups with them.

Now compare this approach to merely presenting an ad that states, "When you are ready to buy or sell a home, give me a call." (Wow, what a sport!)

3. The reason why you ask, through direct mail, email, or social media, all consumers how you can help them is to trigger relationships and to build your real estate ecosystem. Should they want to remodel, you bring in those qualified professionals, and in turn, those professionals (now part of your real estate ecosystem) will refer business to you. Later in the book, I discuss the relationship between building trust and influence, based upon reciprocation.

A. This ensures that when they do decide to sell, the odds of you being contacted to be involved in both transactions is substantially increased. Especially if you develop that which we have developed for our network, "Move, Improve or Relocate" off and online brochures.

B. By bringing in chosen tradespeople, homeowners now feel more trust in you as you have become a part of their all-important real estate-related decision.

C. You will now receive referrals in return from these tradespeople—thus achieving the symbiosis and influence that drives all ecosystems.

4. Let everyone know that your company operates on a regional basis, and you belong to a global network. This, alone, means painting on a larger ecosystem canvas.

5. Disseminate content digitally and physically on all of the above-listed category subjects so that you are now perceived as knowledgeable and connected on all things real estate and lifestyle-related.

6. When asked how the real estate business or market is, do not make declarative and influential killing statements such as: Instead, in order to avoid becoming the living embodiment of what it means to be a real estate lightweight, check out what is preferable to say in the chapter on influential communication. You need to engage consumers in a way that they reveal to you that even if they are not intending to move immediately, there are other home-related services they might need, and this will enable you to continue building your Real Estate Ecosystem.

7. Create and send your real estate services directory (as part of your real estate ecosystem) to all buyers, sellers, and vendors. However, be careful not to promote the directory in such a way that you alienate all of the competitors of your vendors. For example, instead of posting on social media or advertising that a certain landscaper is the very best, just state that you highly recommend them.

8. Let your market/community know that you not only provide excellent service yourself, but you can connect consumers and clients to exceptional vendor/preferred partner services.

9. Create an in-depth, comprehensive community-centric video that simultaneously extolls virtues of not only the schools, parks, transportational convenience, natural and man/woman-made beauty and also the merchants who are the most leverageable as part of your real estate ecosystem. I suggest that in your script you declare, "There are innumerable, outstanding restaurants in town—a couple of great examples are—yet no town offers more reasons to eat out than Springfield." This way, you are highlighting only a few without alienating all others.

Real Estate Ecosystems... Now More Than Ever!

While I hesitate to proclaim that developing one's real estate ecosystem is now more important than ever, as it might sound hyperbolic—unquestionably, this is true. I appreciate that, to many, things within the moment are oftentimes characterized as being "more important than ever"—therefore leading to skepticism. For example, will we ever witness a presidential election where each side does not caution voters that the present election is "the most important in the history of the country?"
Again, at risk of sounding equally sensationalistic, I am convinced that this truly is the most critical time in the history of the real estate industry for real estate profes-

sionals to develop their personal real estate ecosystem. It is because you are presently competing against one of the most highly developed ecosystems mankind has ever constructed - search engines, artificial intelligence, and, of course, Google. Internet-based and artificial intelligence-algorithmic-based ecosystems will only grow much stronger as they compete against your range, reach, influence, and, therefore, your value. Such web-based ecosystems were never a concern of your real estate ancestors.

Google and third-party real estate portals, for example, did not disintermediate the real estate industry. Instead they only disrupted it, and then only on the buying-side. Now the only place that third-party portals can go to increase their real estate-related traffic, and monetize so-called eyeballs, is to cause homesellers to go to the web to select their listing agent.

Since homesellers only move on average every ten years, this means ten more years of homesellers using the internet's ecosystem to search for remodeling, solar panel advice, how to appeal property taxes, to put in a new kitchen, and increasingly—how to select the appropriate real estate listing agent.

Undeniably, when looking to sell, homeowners will increasingly be informed that they can now select the right real estate agent based upon what they charge versus their value. If you are a real estate professional, you are competing with the most pervasive ecosystem of all time regarding consumer engagement—that would be the internet. Unless real estate professionals, in my view, develop personal real estate ecosystems—where the informational value to consumers goes beyond a 'Google Search'—then the first point of contact with homesellers will be forever altered. The real estate industry will increasingly be in a content competition with an informational juggernaut, namely the internet, which not only disseminates information on proverbial steroids but where such content and focus will increaingly be directed towards homesellers prior to their listing descision.

Without your real estate ecosystem, listing-side disruption will encourage value diminution.

It is vitally important that you create sustainable influence during the ten-year period between transactions. Also, I believe your ecosystem is essential to closing the real estate loyalty gap.To close the loyalty gap will mean not only influencing homesellers but also influencing those who influence homesellers and using your influence with homeowners to influence vendors within the community and the friends of the homeowner. This will ensure that when a transactional need does finally emerge, you will naturally be called upon to be their real estate agent, along with receiving innumerable transactional referrals from vendors and their friends and their friends and their friends. Anybody interested in creating a valuable real estate ecosystem should not only list everybody they know but should subsequently make a list of everybody that the primary person knows.

One of the reasons why congresspeople are routinely re-elected over 95% of the time is that they induce people not only to vote for them but to place signs, knock on doors, post, and make phone calls so as to influence others in the community to follow suit. There is no greater example of how to influence influencers than what we see in the political realm. Without question, we will experience an ever-accelerated and intensified competition in terms of where consumers will look to receive their real estate influence. Will it be from third-party websites, financial planners, attorneys, neighbors, family and friends, social media platforms, or will it be you who appropriates and subsumes all of these other forces?

It is imperative that each and every source of influence is first influenced by you. Moving forward, it will not be enough for you to merely join other platforms and networks to optimize your influence. You will need to create and lead a real estate network, a real estate ecosystem. The manner by which you influence consumers through Realtor.com, social media, other professional groups, and every other category within your real estate ecosystem, will for you as an individual, determine if you are to win your local real estate influence competition. As an industry, the degree to which influence is gained and sustained through the development of value-rich, real estate ecosystems will determine whether the next decade becomes the "Age of Real Estate Influence" or the "Age of Real Estate Diminution."

By developing, sustaining, and compellingly influencing consumers through real estate ecosystems, we
will together make the "Age of Real Estate Influence"
a reality.

Chapter 3—
"There's Trouble in Real Estate City"
The Real Estate Loyalty Gap

"There's trouble in River City" is the seminal saying in the memorable musical The Music Man – a play presently being revived for Broadway starring the multi-talented Hugh Jackman. That one legendary line sets the stage for this enduring theatrical gem. The "trouble" (which professor Harold Hill, a traveling con-man reveals to the overly trusting Iowans of fictional River City) was the presence of a pool table in their town. Hill warned that the pool table would corrupt the children of this early 1900's conservative mid-west community. The flamboyant Harold Hill emphatically suggested the need for a boys band which would distract town teenagers, and especially the boys, from all temptations. Unfortunately, his true motive was to sell band instruments he never intended to be delivered.

My metaphorical announcement, "There's trouble in Real Estate City", does not represent a con job. Supportive evidence, in fact, comes from no less a credible source than the National Association of Realtors®. According to NAR research, 90% of consumers indicate that they intend to return to their former real estate agent the next time they buy or sell a home. Yet, according to this survey results, only approximately 12% actually return to their former agent. This void, or as I call it, the real estate loyalty gap, represents potential trouble. That is, unless the real estate industry becomes more relevant, valued, trusted, and influential between real estate transactions. How does one explain this pronounced loyalty gap? Could it be any lower?

I can't imagine many other professions saddled with such a stark absence of loyalty. Sadly, due to societal failure, more released prisoners return to prison than clients and consumers return to their real estate agent.

How does one explain such a dismal track record pertaining to sustaining consumer loyalty? It can't be because real estate agents do not desire repeat business. I am also sure the loyalty gap isn't caused by real estate agents deliberately offending their past clients—not hosting client appreciation parties or including them in their personal promotion celebrations. Granted, a part of the loyalty gap can be attributed to real estate clients moving out of state. Let's also not forget the appreciable numbers of agents leaving the business. What cannot be overlooked in any serious examination of what causes a real estate loyalty gap is the manner in which real estate professionals engage and influence their clients before, during, and after transactions. An unmistakable contributor to the real estate loyalty gap is the lingering consumer perception that real estate agents are only interested in a temporary transaction. Loyalty suffers in the absence of a sustainable relationship—one based upon relevance, timely and topical content, and the establishment of trust, loyalty, and friendship. Additionally, there is a need to illuminate consumers that real estate professionals are not merely interchangeable and non-differentiated commodities.

Regarding what I am referring to as "real estate's loyalty gap," I believe that much of the real estate industry is in denial or disproportionately dismisses the scale of this loyalty issue. Evidence of my assertion that the real estate industry is underestimating how future listing-side transactions will be partially disrupted due to this pronounced loyalty gap was revealed during a recent keynote speech. During my presentation, I asked the audience of six thousand convention attendees to shout out their estimates of what percentage of their clients return to them for future business. The lowest percentage shouted out was 70%. Perhaps these estimated percentages volunteered from the convention floor, which contradicted the research on this subject of real estate loyalty, were skewed.

It might have been that the responses were only offered from our network's most successful agents, those who have mastered the art of engendering greater client loyalty. My research and brokerage experience contradict these high estimates. Real estate agents, in general, devote considerably more time, effort, attention, and money, seeking to acquire new customers and clients than in serving and gaining loyalty from their past clients. This disproportionate focus on securing new customers versus generating referrals from past customers validates that there is trouble in Real Estate City—moving forward.

The audience was disquieted as I related my research that real estate agents collectively spend approximately twenty times as much of their well-deserved compensation seeking to acquire new business from strangers who are disconnected from their sphere of influence, rather than investing in what Allan Dalton prescribes; that being, "influencing one's sphere."

Even though many real estate thought leaders talk incessantly about disruption, there is a different "D-word" that is going unnoticed—and that is "distraction." Since my speech was delivered in Las Vegas, giving me access to that venue's theatrical talent, I arranged for a magician to join me on the Caesar's Colosseum stage. His demonstration was designed to illustrate that distraction is the basis for how all magic works. The magician's performance dramatically reinforced, in a fun-filled fashion, how much of the real estate industry is unwittingly and punitively being distracted. While this strategic stunt was entertaining, it was also edifying to all those in the audience who take a statistical approach to their business. My message was most appreciated by those agents and brokers who reminded me of the Socrates quote, "An unexamined life is not worth living." Similarly, there are thousands of agents who believe an unexamined career is not worth having. These are the real estate professionals who are dedicated to knowing what works and what does not work. Agents whose professional behavior coincided with our convention theme—"All In." Accomplished real estate professionals take very seriously statistics that support my premise that the industry is being distracted by an ill-advised focus on disruption versus value diminution, made worse by the real estate loyalty gap phenomenon and syndrome.

To make my case for how wide-spread distraction is keeping the focus away from what is more relevant to real estate success, I cited examples of where great organizations direct their time and money. These consumer-centric companies concentrate more upon developing and sustaining greater customer loyalty versus being unduly distracted by lackluster and economically imprudent efforts surrounding new customer acquisition. I pointed to how real estate agents spend approximately 20% of their revenue, attempting to acquire new customers. To the contrary, Nike, in order to "Just Do It," spends only 9.6% of their revenue to acquire new customers. Marriott has learned that it is more prudent to reward their present clients than to seek the rewards of new customers. In fact, if you were to ask somebody to identify which word they believe immediately follows the word Marriott, I am confident that many would say "rewards." This emphasis upon rewarding clients is reflected by Marriott only spending 3.2% of their revenue on acquiring new customers. The Nordstrom Way means spending 1.6% of their revenue attracting new customers, while South West Airlines would rather have their present clients appreciate that they "have friends in high places" by spending only 1% to seek new passengers. Why is there such a disparity between how these iconic marketing leaders distinguish between generating customer loyalty and acquiring new customers with how the real estate industry establishes its marketing priorities? These businesses are not as distracted by the shiny object, which is new customers. It is clear that they are disproportionately focused on repeat and referral business. The majority of their business results from what is now referred to as "raving fans". Regrettably, much of the real estate industry devotes most of its effort and money seeking to attract new customers.

Strategic influencing must
transcend perpetual prospecting.

This transformation will place the highest emphasis on serving, sustaining, and generating referrals from past clients. Concentrating on customer and client loyalty prevents distraction, value diminution, and disruption. Before I go further, I want to acknowledge real estate's forward-thinking and most consumer and client-centric real estate professionals – those agents who work each day to assure that their clients return to them. Such professionals have not allowed for a real estate loyalty gap to occur within their careers. I also want to acknowledge that a newcomer to the real estate profession, and especially one without possessing an organic sphere of influence, does not always have the time to emphasize client cultivation and the generation of referrals as their more immediate need is heavy-duty off and online prospecting.

For those who are blessed, however, with robust spheres of influence and existing clients—who have worked arduously in their develpoment—I now want to address another example of distraction caused by deception. I must respectfully say that many real estate professionals deceive themselves when confusing the difference between having 100% of their business generated from their sphere of influence versus their sphere of influence share. Let's assume that one's database is comprised of one thousand homeowners. Since homeowners move on average every ten years, this suggests that one hundred homes will be sold in a particular year. Therefore, should an agent close fifteen homeseller transactions in that year, this result would represent only a 15% sphere of influence share. A 15% sphere of influence share sounds and is dramatically different (thus the deception and distraction) than when boasting that "100% of

one's business is generated from a sphere of influence."
I refer to this 15% versus 100% number as an example of
one's IQ or "influence quotient"—regarding sphere of influence success. These IQ statistics, again, inform us that
if 100% of one's business is from a database or sphere
of influence (but it only represents 15% of the business
within that sphere), then there is much more potential to
be realized through elevated influence. Moreover, given
the 85% of non-converted sphere of influence business,
along with how 100% of one's total business came from
that sphere of influence, one must consider how much
more effectively real estate agents should influence their
sphere versus the non-sphere population. Obviously,
you want to have a combination of both sphere-related
business and new business through social media prospecting, yet it is vital to understand which is potentially
the more lucrative. That's why I devoted a chapter in
this book discussing the importance of exponentially increasing one's sphere of influence by developing a thriving and symbiotic real estate ecosystem.

Of additional concern, notwithstanding the billions of
dollars devoted to personal promotion, property promotion, and brand building, the number of real estate
transactions has essentially remained flat over the past
20 years. Moreover, real estate transactions have not
increased, even with a significant increase in population. Therefore, disturbingly, the vast amount of money
directed towards customers and clients apparently does
not stimulate additional transactions.

What better example of either misplaced or underutilized influence? Should the real estate industry accept any responsibility for how consumers currently move on average every 9 to 10 years versus 7 or 8 years in past decades? The reason I cite these statistics is because it is an indictment on how the real estate industry directs its money and attention; and consequently blunts its greater influence. I'd like to revisit the example of when innumerable real estate professionals proclaim that almost all of their business comes from personal referrals and sphere of influence. This fertile and affectionately acknowledged source of business begs the following question: Why is so much more money dedicated to these other non-lucrative sources of advertising, personal promotion, social media, prospecting, and lead generation other than, underwittingly, subsidizing third-party portals and potential strategic disruptors?

Are Real Estate Professionals Devoting More Time to Selling Themselves...Than Real Estate?

The answer might be that the industry at large has been distracted through its seismic effort to sell strangers on its merits versus influencing past clients to buy & sell and refer more real estate with their former agent. Little wonder why this wide-spread distraction has caused so many agents to prospect for new business versus influencing their sphere of influence for referrals and repeat business. Ask yourself how many seminars are devoted to personal promotion, social media, and prospecting (albeit all very important) versus strategies related to either lifetime client development or how to someday sell your business. Perpetual prospecting, and awareness advertising, essentially and inadvertently announces to the market the following:

"I clearly do not have clients that I am in the process of serving. I am, therefore, constantly trolling for prospects. Nobody views me as their agent for life. I am too distracted by prospecting for new clients to spend my time better serving the clients I do possess."

What else could consumers infer when reading advertisements indiscriminately directed towards a community at large that state, "when you are ready to buy or sell a home, give me a call"? This oft-repeated and industry cherished message inadvertently encourages consumers to read between the lines: "Until you are ready to buy or sell a home, don't bother me." Conventional real estate wisdom universally celebrates the axiom that "listings are the name of the game". Greater influence can only occur after the following realization takes place.

Clients are the name of the game—because clients will lead to more listings...and buyers.

Not just because I am from Texas, but success in real estate must take the form of a Texas two-step. Step one is to influence and satisfy consumers and clients. Step two is to sustain their loyalty, leading to many more listing and buying-side referrals. Speaking of creating consumer loyalty, why do so many consumers settle on only one financial planner, dentist, or attorney yet continue to play real estate roulette when contemplating who should be their real estate agent? It is because these other professionals devote and influence building and sustaining a professional and salable "practice" versus merely reminding themselves that they are running a business. Their practices are based upon client loyalty.

44

They clearly differentiate between one-time-only-customers and clients for life. To be fair, I appreciate that there are thousands of real estate professionals who are supremely successful due to their spheres of influence, databases, contact management systems, and high caliber professional service and skills rendered. Yet, the industry, as a whole, must achieve a level of relational influence that matches its transactional readiness. There is a reason why doctors, lawyers, dentists, and other professionals can sell their practices more successfully than hard-working and very accomplished real estate professionals can sell their personal "business". It has to do with the very nature of how these other professionals engage, influence, and establish relevance and indispensability, far beyond a Google search. Without question, their professional practices are strategic. This is in contrast to the more transactionally tactical real estate structure. Without appreciating the profound distinction between how transactions are tactical, and relationships are strategic, influence cannot be optimized.

Top real estate professionals, who expect to withstand partial listing-side disruption, will have to exponentially increase their level of influence. Optimizing influence will require expanding beyond conventional client appreciation events, the present use of social networking platforms, and traditional geographical farming methods.

A career of high-level consumer and client influence must begin when real estate agents first enter the profession. They must, before listing everyone they have ever known, first learn and identify that which makes them valuable, indispensable, and therefore influential. Most agents, upon entering the real estate industry, are asked to write out on paper or in their computer the names of everyone they know and hopefully the names of everyone their acquaintances know. In order to create loyalty for life, the practice of identifying and building a sphere of influence, and then a database, must be in concert with developing an appreciation of how their differentiated value can serve and influence everyone within their sphere and within the real estate markets they work. Without identifying markets, along with deciding how to personally influence them, the wrong attitude is developed and perpetuated. That being, that success has more to do with popularity and visibility than through professional influence.

Beyond spheres of influence, so-called geographical farms are worthless in the absence of high-level value and influence. We have all heard the joke, "if a consumer does not have a friend in real estate, it is likely that they are friendless." My colleague Allan Dalton aptly says, "real estate professionals must convert databases to client bases" and that real estate agents have been "farming for years, but unfortunately planting the wrong seeds". I completely agree. The "wrong seeds" planted, in my view, are due to a lack of consumer-centric content.

Moreover, real estate agents need to be able to better influence their social media followers, their geographical farm populations, and strategic spheres of influence through the passional propagation of unmistakable value, superior service, remarkable skills, pronounced knowledge, and wisdom—all leading to elevated influence. In turn, elevated influence (rather than merely prospecting, networking, visibility campaigns, social media, event marketing, etc.) will ultimately be what closes the real estate loyalty gap through effectively addressing the real estate industry's 'value void.'

Chapter 4—
Trust and Influence

How often, if ever, have you been involved in negotiating a real estate transaction and the real estate agent representing the other client disclosed sensitive information which you believed violated their client's trust and possibly the Realtor® code of ethics?

When I ask this question of real estate professionals during my speeches, almost every single hand in the audience affirms that they have experienced breaches of professional trust amongst industry colleagues. The immediate and resonant condemnation from most of the audience to this provocative and unanticipated question leaves me wondering if it is appropriate or accurate for each and every real estate professional to promote themselves as a real estate trusted advisor or, said another way, a Trusted Real Estate Advisor.

My concern over the potential widespread and indiscriminate redefining of the role of a real estate professional was best expressed when Shakespeare wrote in Hamlet, "suit the action to the word, and the word to the action." Or, as I like to say in my speeches, the 'do' must match the 'tell.'

At its most basic level, proclamations of trust must be validated in actuality, not just categorically announced.

For example, there may be some real estate agents who believe that when representing a homeseller, and without their approval, disclosing to a buyer agent that their clients are divorcing is appropriate. Divulging this information without client authorization constitutes a violation of both ethics and trust. Yet even after this violation of trust, there are some real estate agents who still show no hesitation in defining themselves as a trusted real estate advisor. Another example of when actions do not suit the word 'trust' is when a real estate professional throughout their career continually fabricates to buyer agents, and thus their buyers, that they have received multiple offers.

Regarding the example of the inappropriate disclosure of a client's divorce, all one has to do is revisit Article 1 of the Realtor® Code of Ethics, which states that Realtors® have a fiduciary responsibility to their clients, and they and their clients are to be viewed as one. Therefore, that agent must ask themself, if they were the homeseller, would they want this information divulged? If so, they should first ask the homeowners if this information should be shared as part of the overall marketing and negotiation strategy and present the pros and cons of such a non-disclosure required revelation.

In the case where it is considered to be in the best interest of the homesellers in order to stimulate activity and then hold firm on price in negotiations, the voluntary disclosure I believe should be along the following lines: "My clients are going through a divorce and have given me permission to share this information." This way, the buyer agent trusts the ethics of the selling agent. The buyer, in turn, trusts the agent representing the seller and therefore is likely to trust more the overall transactional real estate process and profession in general. These buyers may also remember how professionally and ethically this information was handled and, in the future, when they look to sell their next home, this recollection will become a factor in the selection process. Ethics builds trust, trust builds influence, and influence builds future business.

I am addressing the relationship between trust and influence, during an era where there is an exponential increase in the number of real estate agents throughout the globe proclaiming themselves to be trusted real estate advisors. This industry trend towards seeking greater trust from consumers, given its widespread velocity, calls for a need to fully grasp the relationship between gaining greater trust and developing greater real estate influence.

As I often mention in my talks, in the Information Age, information and data possess less influence than knowledge and wisdom. Since data and information are now ubiquitous and conveniently accessible to everyone, generating trust and influence from these two elements of the real estate decision-making process alone is increasingly difficult. Consequently, the knowledge and wisdom possessed by real estate agents, and thus the trust they engender and influence they wield, must now become the two elements possessing paramount importance.

The industry intuitively understands that their real and perceived value must now go beyond both the data and the transaction. The acceptance of this transitional need explains the collective and professional pull towards announcing one's value in the form of being a real estate trusted advisor and not merely a real estate agent. While this is prudent, one intended for consumers to accept this elevated and expanded real estate agent definition and role, it will require, for such a lofty designation to be accepted, more than mere words or a shift in title. It is significant that the higher value of agents, now contingent upon their indispensable knowledge and wisdom, becomes the justification or rationale behind the new professional definition. One all-important aspect of what will be required to cause a similar fondness amongst consumers towards the words 'trusted real estate advisor' as that of 'agents' will be to better ensure that real estate professionals are trusted not just because of their personal and professional integrity, but also for their knowledge, wisdom and exceptional competency.

Since trust is inextricable with creating influence, let's first define the term. A general definition of trust among many, which I embrace, is that trust is believing that the person you trust will do what is expected. If one is proclaiming to provide trusted advice, then the advice must indeed be trustworthy and verifiable. While there are innumerable yet similar other definitions of trust, there seems to be complete unanimity surrounding its epic significance. That trust begins at birth enjoys the consensus of most psychological experts. The brain of a baby immediately learns that she or he can trust being fed when hungry and loved and nurtured by fellow humans, primarily the mother. Scientists have concluded that the trust a baby develops through the parent and child cooperation process is indispensable to the development and success of our species. The trust and cooperation process is also indispensable to the real estate process.

Economists collectively view trust as the cohesiveness necessary to drive and sustain our entire economy. Who amongst us would use a bank, buy a stock, or accept a check without trust? We are indeed all profoundly influenced by trust.

The sharing, reciprocation, and cooperation of all societies are governed by trust. And not just we humans. I remember learning in my bioscience classes of the trust that exists in animal groups who share food with each other, when some animals in their group have no food, and how this leads to reciprocal trust. There also had to be trust during earlier generations of hunters in order to exchange berries for meat for mutual satisfaction. Moreover, fishermen and farmers must trust that their products will be bought at market. Societal groups function optimally when a groundwork of trust exists between members.

Earlier in this book I wrote about the importance of establishing real estate-related ecosystems. Such systems are not possible to sustain without trust. To begin a process of generating trust, and thus influence, means understanding the distinction between personal and professional trust. One connotation of trust is when people trust your personal integrity and character. The other type of trust, is trust surrounding an estimation of the professional probability of your ability to provide value and results. The difference between personal and professional trust can be illustrated by the example of having a twin brother or sister whom you trust more than any other person on a personal level, but whom you would not trust to fly you in an airplane, due to a low anticipation of probable success. Or the football player I knew back in Texas, who was always trying to cheat on the football field but who went on to become a trusted professional pilot. The person whom I trust more than all others is Monica, my wife. Yet, I do not trust Monica as much as myself to teach my son Austin techniques to play better basketball. As simple as these trust-related distinctions are, it is vital that there be complete clarity between what distinguishes personal and professional trust from each other, as well as what qualities they have in common.

With the vast implications of trust and its indispensable role in society, I am sure it does not surprise you that there are countless explanations for the establishment of trust. There are three distinct levels of personal trust and professional trust. Randy Conley, who writes and speaks of trust on a national level, suggests there are three levels of trust: deterrence-based trust, knowledge-based trust, and identity-based trust. Let us explore how these three levels impact real estate.

Deterrence-based trust is indispensable to almost all societal interaction, including real estate. Consumers trust the fact that legal considerations and the professional code of ethics deter real estate professionals from harming them in general. Why else would complete strangers trust visiting open houses, invite unknown professionals into their homes, or drive through unfamiliar communities with real estate agents they have never met before? While this first level of where trust is established is not inspiring, let us all be extremely grateful that deterrence-based trust exists. How else could it be understood throughout society that there are severe consequences for breaching trust, when harming others physically or financially?

Knowledge-based trust regarding real estate influence is based upon the insight others gain after getting to know you. This is why throughout this book I stress the importance of developing personal relationships. I remind my network agents during my speeches and broadcasts of the NAR research that revealed that 75 percent of homesellers interview only one agent. This means, in most cases, that an agent had already established a relationship based upon knowledge and trust. Simply put, the clients most likely had an opportunity to get to know that real estate agent over time before selecting them as their current real estate agent. Perhaps the homesellers felt no loyalty to the agent they knew from a previous real estate transaction because they only perceive them as a transactionally-focused agent. Managing a real estate transaction successfully does not by itself close the loyalty gap. Instead, when a real estate agent leverages the transaction process and uses it as a platform to launch a longer-term and sustainable relationship based on trust, only then will the real estate loyalty gap be closed.

The third level of trust, according to Conley—one which I believe has the greatest nexus to creating and sustaining influence—is trust based upon identity or intimacy. When you have identified and shown empathy regarding the real estate goals, lifestyle dreams, and present-day circumstances of those with whom you seek to gain trust, you are now operating at the highest level of trust—and therefore influence.

These three proposed levels of trust however, do not fully identify how to gain this intimate level of personal or professional trust. Within each of these three levels, there are endless elements for developing trust within those three categories of trust.

I have chosen what I consider to be some indispensable building blocks for trust:

1. Respect

2. Shared values

3. Integrity

4. Transparency

5. Concern for others

6. Empathy

7. Reciprocation

8. Competency

9. Accountability

Here is how I interpret the connection between these nine steps and the acquisition of trust. Let us review them one at a time:

1. Respect
Can you think of anybody that you trust that either you do not respect, or they do not respect you? I am sure your answer is "no."

2. Shared values
Let us see which of these two messages you believe coincides with developing greater trust and influence through shared values:

Ads which read—
   I am number 1,
   Discover the Chris Stuart difference,
   Spouses selling houses,
   The home team,
   When you are ready to buy or sell your home, give me a call.
Or—
   I sell America's best lifestyle, Lake Tahoe,
   Marketing Lake Tahoe Real Estate at the highest level,
   Let's keep Lake Tahoe safe.

Clearly, by connecting yourself to the shared values of all residents and particularly homeowners you immediately establish one step of the trust pyramid.

3. Integrity

Integrity is keeping your word and your personal character. Consumers are always evaluating the integrity of profession-als with whom they come in contact, both personally and professionally.

Therefore, it is always important that real estate agents, while attending social functions, never overlook the reality that while other guests are only being judged socially you are also and always being judged professionally. Remember, your integrity is always on display.

4. Transparency

Trust and transparency go together like a swimming pool and water. How can anyone secure trust when there is a lack of transparency? A primary explanation of consum-ers' historically low rankings of agent trust goes back to the pre-internet.

Many real estate companies included in their training programs, years ago, the following advice pertaining to transparency. The recommendation was that when a buyer calls about an ad and asks for information about the property— don't provide it. Instead, probe the prospective buyer for information about them. As an example, when a buyer asked, "Does the home have four bedrooms?" rather than simply responding, "Yes, the property does have four bedrooms, what else would you like to know?" Instead, and astoundingly, real estate professionals were trained to answer with, "Do you want four bedrooms?" We have all heard the expression that absolute power corrupts absolutely. In the days before Realtor.com and Zillow, the real estate industry had complete power over the dissemination of consumer-relevant information.

Unfortunately, such power became deployed in an ill-advised, trust-killing, and nonsensical sales ploy versus opting for transparency. This is why I am including transparency as one of my nine cornerstones in developing real estate-related trust.

5. Concern for others
Please always keep in mind as you drive safely through your community, especially if you have an advertisement on your automobile, that you demonstrate concern for others. One cannot gain enduring trust if one does not consistently convey a concern for all others. Anyone who reveals callousness or disrespect for other professionals, their colleagues, or actually any other category of people demonstrates that they should not be trusted. Trust is violated here in the same way as when you observe someone speaking disrespectfully about

someone not present at a group dinner. Such behavior can cause you to consider waiting until you get home, instead of excusing yourself to use the restroom. The expectation is that if a person exhibits such behavior once, it is quite possibly their typical behavior. I've always appreciated the saying 'when Peter talks about Paul; he actually tells you more about Peter.'

Another trust-killer would be if a consumer ever gets a sense that a real estate agent is more concerned for the transaction outcome than the client. An example of when trust is possibly injured over a questionable concern for clients occurs when countless agents say to homesellers, when presenting their first offer, "Well, oftentimes the first offer is the best offer." Consumers are much more likely to hear this comment from their agent than, "Oftentimes the first offer is the worst offer." Without any documented science behind this assertion, it is to be expected that some homesellers might wonder if they are being prematurely encouraged to sell quickly due to a realization by the agent that if the homeowner does not accept this first offer, the home might not sell and they may not get paid.

Now, while this explanation might also speak to the agent's concern for their client, it can also clumsily ignore the other reality. In a classic example of how 'the stand that one takes depends on where one sits'—the homesellers want the highest possible price and are willing to push the price envelope. They may also sense that the agent is less willing to push for a twenty-five thousand dollar additional offer—which might generate, after their negotiated compensation, splits that only generate a much smaller additional level of compensation, yet to the homeowner perhaps an additional twenty-three or twenty-four thousand dollars is immensely and disproportionately different. Clearly, should the home not sell during the listing agreement timetable, there are different consequences for the agent and homeseller, which should be transcended by Article 1 of the Realtor® Code of Ethics. This is why it is understandable that some agents might create a sense that they and their clients have different agendas. All the more reason for an agent to never induce any belief that there is not a deep sense of concern for their clients. Otherwise, this is known as 'confirmation biased.' That being that some homesellers believe that real estate agents are more concerned with their commission than their client's financial outcome. To avoid this occurrence, I suggest the following. During your marketing presentation when you bring up your negotiating game plan, point this out, "Folks, when I present offers, let me say now, sometimes the offer will be, in my view, the best offer we might receive, and I will explain why—and sometimes it will be the worst offer."

This balance of expectations will ensure that the homeseller will not inevitably assume that when a real estate agent says, "the first offer is often the best offer," that they are just motivated by selfish convenience, which undermines trust.

6. Empathy

I realize that concern for others and empathy may appear to be one and the same. To me, the difference is 'concern for others' means a level of concern for humanity directed towards everybody. Empathy, to me, represents an intense personal regard for an individual and their circumstances. We can never listen to the concerns of the whole world with the same degree of focus and empathy, as when we are meeting with one or more individuals. We have all heard the expression, "Nobody cares how much you know until they know how much you care." This, to me, aptly summarizes empathy.

7. Reciprocation

It is common within real estate circles to hear, in seminars, from coaches, and in everyday banter, references to the principle of reciprocity. If I do something for you, you will be more motivated to do something for me. When this concept is not fully appreciated, it leads to overtly selfish behavior.

Consider this difference, as I mentioned elsewhere in the book. When a real estate agent puts on the back of their business card, ***"The sincerest compliment one can pay me is to send me referrals of their family and friends"***, this does not suggest any reciprocal benefit; therefore the opportunity to build trust suffers. Conversely, if the back of the card were to read, ***"My greatest professional privilege is to serve the real estate needs of your family and friends."*** It suggests reciprocation. You do something for me because I will do something for your friends and family. It is similar to the difference between asking people for their loyalty, which is about you, versus thanking someone for their loyalty, which is about them, and which creates and rewards greater loyalty.

8. Competency is the next stage of acquiring and sustaining trust. This speaks for itself.

9. Accountability

When consumers and clients know that you are accountable for your promises and that you are reliable in everything you say, then trust soars. No one I know embodies accountability more than Gino Blefari, the CEO of HomeServices of America. I have also never known anyone more effective in causing others to accept accountability than is Gino. For Gino to have the opportunity to prove his exceptional accountability measures, he had to first establish trust based upon mutual respect, shared values, integrity, concern for others, empathy, transparency, reciprocation, and competency.

He would also say the reverse is true—that if he were not completely accountable, all the other steps of developing trust would have been nullified.

An amazing component of trust that I learned in my research is that the brain receives pleasure both when we trust others and when we believe that we have earned the trust of others. A note of concern that speaks to a completely different emotion is that revenge caused by a breach of trust also can provide pleasure. In this age of ratings and reviews, make sure you do not generate negative influence directed towards you by providing any consumers or clients the pleasure of exacting revenge against you for not being trustworthy in what you say and do.

While gaining trust leads to influence, it does not automatically generate influence. Gordon Tredgold, founder and CEO of Leadership Principles, makes this very point by elucidating 9 keys for turning trust into influence:

1. By delivering results
2. By coaching others
3. Through consistency
4. Through honesty
5. With openness
6. With humbleness
7. Through evangelizing
8. Through human kindness
9. With bravery

My favorite of these nine is to be an evangelist. Consumers and clients gravitate to agents who not only love what they do but also convey that they are supreme believers in the importance of owning real estate. Trust and influence come oftentimes when someone is selling something bigger and other than themselves. People trust clergy because they speak of beliefs greater than themselves. To gain the trust that will lead to the Age of Real Estate Influence will mean more than just announcing that one is to be trusted.

In 2012, the Journal of Experimental Social Psychology conducted research on trust. They asked subjects to believe that they were thieves, grifters, and swindlers. They then asked the subjects to attempt to influence someone to buy their product by first gaining their trust. They found that these subjects took a different approach than another group of subjects who were told they were trustworthy. The group who internalized that they were crooks made it a point to overly smile and overly touch, and also repeatedly pointed out that they could be trusted. This research raises the following question. We generally do not find other professionals constantly advertising and promoting that they are the attorneys you can trust or, "Call me. I am a trusted doctor or engineer." Please consider what the impact will be amongst consumers when real estate agents enthusiastically and continuously broadcast that they are to be trusted. Is there a risk that this declaration may create a general sense that the highest value of real estate agents is now that they should be trusted?

The reason why it is unlikely that you will observe a law firm boasting of how their practice consists of 'trusted attorneys' or a university announcing that their entire faculty is comprised of 'trusted professors,' is that, presumably, trust in these others professions is already inferred by the public. Regarding psychiatrists, it ostensibly is implicit in agency that you legally or ethically can trust your therapist not to share your personal trials or transgressions with the public at large. Confidentiality is presumed. In other words, people assume professional trust, and if it must be held up as a virtue to be saluted, this could trigger a countervailing concern. At the very least, it injects the notion of distrust within the industry at large as it overtly cautions consumers to be wary of all those real estate professionals who cannot be trusted. This careless and ill-advised attempt at differentiation, without question, undermines the influence and reputation of the entire real estate industry. Therefore, it is critical, at least internally, to separate announcements that speak to how one can be personally trusted versus stating that you can trust my professional knowledge, experience, and advice. If a doctor cheats in a card game yet has performed successful surgeries one hundred percent of the time, they will consequently gain considerable trust and influence based upon their competency.

One cannot examine the relationship between trust and influence without factoring in the immense relevance of the times in which we live. Historians most likely will someday refer to our times as the Information Age. What makes these times the Information Age? It is because the internet and then the web opened the sharing of information to everyone with access to advanced technology.

This phenomenon has been referred to as the democratization of information or citizen journalism. That everyone has an opportunity to now share information, and therefore influence, with the world does not mean that this benefit occurs equally. Some had hoped that the internet would function in the same fashion as a farmers' market.

Every individual and their website, blog, and use of social media platforms would equally benefit from internet-related exposure. The reason this equality of exposure never happened is that unlike a farmers market, whereby most visitors get to peruse each offering, in the same way that real estate agents in most cases, get to visit all convention booths during their 3 days at their annual convention, exposure on the web is much more elusive. Exposure became linked to the strategies and economics surrounding the display of organic or paid content. Not only can the web be a treacherous place where reputations in some cases go to die, there is an ongoing battle or competition between content participants to reach desired audiences. Within this book, I outline which social media platforms I believe are the most effective and economical in increasing your range, reach and influence.

Gaining trust, however, is not the exclusive domain of the digital world. The acquisition of trust is also governed by how you portray your image off and online.

The gaining of trust even extends to how you dress, how you speak, and which colors and words you typically use. For example, research validates that study groups who dress more professionally in case studies negotiate more profitably. Certain words also have incredibly greater influence.

Within this book, you will learn what I believe are the most effective and influential methods of communicating with homesellers, for sale by owners, expired listing homesellers, and buyers.

I review these traditional areas of influence, as if all one had to do is to determine which media buys, social media platforms, or which influencers need to be influenced—then this would undermine ultimate real estate professional value—because it would mean that anyone, even those without any real estate knowledge and trust, could take over your entire real estate business from their basement due alone to their superior understanding and use of social media.

Instead, the Age of Real Estate Influence must mean generating compelling influence both off and online—and by including evidence of your skillful representation of clients and ongoing services. The way in which you use the latest in technology and social media alone to engage consumers, will not determine your ultimate influence and success. I am reminded of what the legendary Jim

Weichert once said, "No consumer has ever shaken hands with an email." That is right. There is no greater expression of human trust than shaking hands on it!

Although during Covid, a legitimate hesitancy to shake hands on a transaction became common, for centuries, many people would not trust a transaction without a handshake.

Even though I often refer to successful real estate professionals as de facto fellow CEOs, please know that according to the Edelman Trust Barometer (based upon a survey of 33,000 people in 28 countries) trust in CEOs, government officials, and leaders is at an all-time low. This trust void provides you with a sizeable opportunity as an individual to fill in this void by generating influence within your community and additional influence through social media channels.

You might want to look at this opportunity in this way. Just as over 85% of citizens distrust Congress in general, over 95% of congresspeople get re-elected. This validates that just as people have a distrust for information, news, people in power, and a wide range of authority figures, they trust most and are influenced greatly by individuals, even more than companies. These are people with whom they have relationships that go beyond the transaction. You should be excited to announce that you are a Real Estate Trusted Advisor, especially when you can be trusted not only based upon your personal integrity but also on your deep, profound, and indispensable knowledge, wisdom, and superior skills. Titles alone do not create trust or influence—professionals like yourself do—for which we can all be grateful.

Chapter 5—
Service, Services, and Skills
in the Age of Real Estate Influence

Before turning my attention to the relationship between effective influence and the optimization of service, services, and skills, I want to ensure that readers of this book fully grasp the difference between devaluation and disruption.

Although seemingly redundant, I harken back to what is the seminal distinction between the two. Over the past several years, for every time the word 'devaluation' or 'diminution' has been uttered, the word 'disruption' has been expressed countless more times. Consequently, the real estate industry has been enraptured with the subject of disruption decidedly more so than devaluation. Although buying-side disruption means that buyers now begin their home search without an agent, this development did not bring with it negative financial consequences. The reason being is that the negotiation of fees has historically and overwhelmingly been the purview of prospective sellers and not the domain of buyers.

Listing-side disruption, like buying-side disruption, fortunately will not lead to the outright displacement of real estate agents. However, partial disruption on the listing-side does pose a considerable threat to the perceived importance of real estate professionals in general. This is because partial listing-side disruption will have impact on perceived value by diminishing what homesellers consider to be appropriate charges for when selling their home through professional marketing. The more that home-sellers begin to search for a listing agent online, the more that this consumer welcomed trend will alter both their selection process and their approach to perceived value. Unless influential relationships between homesellers and real estate agents are established, and therefore preempt internet search for a listing agent, the more that consumers will determine agent selection based upon negotiated costs than value.

Digital disruptors will effectively employ consumer seductive chum line-like bait. Their strategic seduction, seeking to exploit the real estate loyalty gap, will feature advertisements relating to discounts, rebates, and reviews rather than results and value. Their off and online pronouncements will be dedicated to persuading homesellers that their companies now represent the long-awaited arbiters required to finally educate homesellers of which real estate agents represent the greatest bargain and, therefore, the highest level of value.

There may be many so-called 'listing agents' who underestimate the very real possibility of listing side disruption. They do so at their own peril. I don't make that observation in the form of a criticism. Quite possibly, many real estate agents have, figuratively speaking, developed antibodies to the relentless threats of disruption repeatedly expressed over the past decade. Fortunately, despite these lingering threats, top real estate agents have continued to see their businesses flourish unabated.

Any dire prognostication surrounding the word 'disruption' for many has become real estate's version of the boy who called wolf.

I still respectfully suggest that disruption, and particularly partial disruption, and on the listing-side, remains a valid threat. Moreover, listing-side disruption will bring with it decidedly different consequences than the false equivalency of buying-side disruption. This is because the buyer generally does not shop for real estate negotiated value and buyers as we all know, do not generate listings as much as listings generate buyers. Essentially every top producer I know focuses more on securing listings than servicing buyers.

The solution to the possibility of listing-side disruption can be summarized in two words—influence and value. External influence, that which involves the public, can only come after internal influence is first realized.

Professional influence must emanate from the development, recognition, and celebration of one's full value.

One must first believe that she or he possesses the power of influence. Only then will real estate professionals become empowered to truly influence others. Influence and confidence are co-dependent and must work together to transform the way in which consumers perceive the value of real estate professionals. Confidence is also based upon how much value a real estate agent believes that they can deliver. A classic definition regarding the 'laws of compensation' is that compensation is in direct proportion to the quantity and quality of value rendered. Regarding perceived value, I invite you to contemplate the following question. If you were to construct a pie chart and had to delineate proportional pieces of your pie, relative to the value you attribute to each component of your overall value, what would it look like?

What Percentage of Your 'Value Pie' Would You Attribute to...

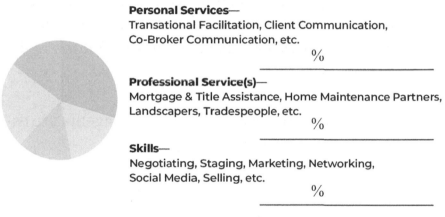

Personal Services—
Transational Facilitation, Client Communication, Co-Broker Communication, etc.
%
_____

Professional Service(s)—
Mortgage & Title Assistance, Home Maintenance Partners, Landscapers, Tradespeople, etc.
%
_____

Skills—
Negotiating, Staging, Marketing, Networking, Social Media, Selling, etc.
%
_____

What percentage of your Value Pie is from your
Professional Service, Your Value Added Service and/or Professional Skills?

What percentage of your pie would you attribute to the additional services your company provides? What percentage would be based upon your personal service?

Lastly, what would be the percentage that your professional skills represent? The reason I encourage this value-related exercise is multi-fold. Rather than merely encouraging you to simply proclaim that you give great service is not sufficient.

Instead, greater value must be conveyed to preempt listing side diminution, or partial disruption (versus full disruption), especially due to the following concerns:

1. Many consumers perceive real estate fees across the board (although all industry fees are negotiable) as value incongruent.

2. There will be greater legal and consumer focus and transparency on whether the real estate industry inappropriately coordinates industry-wide fees. I don't believe this concern is true.

3. Many consumers believe that real estate agents are essentially alike regarding how they perform.

Therefore, to countervail consumer perception and to establish professional differentiation I would hope that everyone associated with the real estate industry would be dedicated to providing the highest of value, and let what consumers are willing to pay fall where it may.

Regarding perceived value—based upon the importance of service—I have never heard of a real estate agent who, upon meeting a prospective client, cautioned them by announcing, "Just so you know, I do not provide good service." In other words is there a real estate professional on the globe that does not profess they give good service?

Given how, at times, the delusional and low bar required regarding declarations of great or full-service and the relationship of these terms with what truly constitutes full-service, I want to share my perspective regarding the definitions and distinctions pertaining to service, services, and skills.

Let's begin by defining 'service' and its relationship to professional skills. Countless real estate professionals, when challenged on their suggested and negotiable fees from homesellers, have responded with the following defense or justification—"While I can appreciate that the other agent is offering to sell your home for less, I give better service." Does this proclamation really resonate when perceived consumers have difficulty distinguishing differentiation and value from one agent to another? Or, does this response fall flat among homesellers in relation to one's perception of the value surrounding the so-called service sector?

Let's examine the way in which other service sector industries are perceived by consumers regarding value. When one purchases an automobile, the car salesperson may deliver numerous test drives, explain in great detail the mechanical nuances of various automobiles, arrange financing, and follow-up with additional information. All of these behaviors, in many cases, do not appear to change the following interpretation of a car salesperson's role. It is not unusual for a satisfied customer, after their purchase, to comment to a friend, "Hey, if you are going to buy a new car, go see Sally. She's a GREAT SALESPERSON." The attribution to Sally being a great salesperson trumps, "If you are buying a car, you have got to meet Sally. She provides great service." This distinction between sales or service attribution, regarding value, is that the consumer intuitively and experientially, understands that all of the behavior exhibited by Sally was due to her motive to sell the car. Additionally, her ultimate motivation is perceived to be that of receiving a 'sales' commission. A year later, that same automobile consumer confirms that they know the difference between selling and service by saying, "Hey, if you are buying a car, you need to call my friend Sally. She is a great salesperson, and they also have a fantastic service department." The challenge that the entire real estate industry faces, moving forward, is one that will require rigorous examination. That is, while the real estate industry prides itself on providing exceptional service, as well as possessing valuable skills, there is a not a suitable effort surrounding helping consumers to separate the two.

While there may be an expectation that consumers will recognize and reward this combined value, how then does one explain such low overall industry ratings? In order to gain greater influence and respect, I believe will require a disproportionate focus on skills versus service and a flipping of the 'value cake.' For years, baked into real estate value, was that service was the main ingredient.

That must change by causing consumers to better understand that real estate skills reflect the cake, and service is the frosting..and not the reverse.

Clearly, there is a marked difference between all that is entailed in marketing and selling a home, with its almost unfathomable complexity and the protracted period of time involved in consummating a real estate transaction, with the relative simplicity of selling an automobile. There is demonstrably less value and skill involved in selling an automobile—just as there is in selling a stock. Unlike a real estate professional, the car salesperson does not have to develop marketing, negotiating, staging, networking, appreciable administrative skills, or have to negotiate with the parties representing the other side of the transaction. Yet, there is a lesson to be learned from this asymmetrical comparison. When buyers are shown innumerable properties over many days, many weeks, and are continually updated with emails, links to other homes, and receive financing, appraisal, and escrow direction from their agent, this is considered great service. So too, when the agent brings a dehumidifier for a homeseller client's damp basement, brings in a stager or landscaper, or supremely talented photographer (who incidentally is valued more for their skills than service), all of these activities are often perceived more as a component of good salespersonship, and not even remarkable service. What is taking place is that all these services are considered part of the selling process, and additionally, not even being promoted as skills. The real estate industry, in this regard, is in a sort of no man's land regarding value. Where service is under-appreciated as it is expected, and professional skills go either unrecognized or undervalued. If every action a real estate agent performs during the transactional process is considered as either outstanding service or a perfunctory part of the sales process, how then should the following actions be defined: staging, marketing, negotiating, networking, advertising, social media, professional communication, trending data reports, knowledge and administrative vigilance?

To me, these activities represent skills and not service. How about you? If all of these activities commonly referred to as "servicing the listing" represent outstanding service, when does the value of real estate skills come in? The reason why the real estate industry has been able to distinguish itself, for decades, from 'for sale by owners' is not based upon the value of one's service but instead based upon the value of one's services and skills.

__Astonishingly and uniquely, the real estate industry may very well be the only profession that actually downplays its value.__

It does so by collectively characterizing valuable skills as merely routine services. Little wonder why so many consumers regard real estate professionals in lower esteem than is warranted. How could they not, as the real estate industry has seemingly undermined all of its transactional value and influence by advocating the wrong category of value—service versus skills. One should not be surprised that due to this self-minimalization of skills (and services), that consumers have followed suit and in-turn commoditized real estate professional value. This commoditization is caused when there is a prevailing belief that real estate professionals represent a sector of undifferentiated service providers versus members of an elite profession distinguished by highly skilled practitioners. This also explains why I believe that when consumers experience a legal or medical need, they are more likely to be told, "You better get a good lawyer or doctor," more than being told as frequently, "If you are buying or selling a home, you had better get a good real estate agent."

Within the skill sector, there is a clearer distinction between highly appreciated services and much higher value skills.

We all place a higher value, if not always appreciation, for the difference between pilots and flight attendants, chefs and waiters, and not just the difference between attorneys and paralegals, and also doctors and orderlies. One of the reasons why so many consumers consider all real estate professionals to be one and the same is because real estate service can appear to be routine and commoditized, such as MLS, the internet, a for sale sign, open houses, and ads reading: 4 bedrooms, 2 ½ baths, professionally landscaped and park-like setting. On the other hand, the more that consumers are appropriately influenced regarding your skillful use of the internet, the skillful marketing of an open house, your skillful and compelling ad writing, the skill involved in staging, negotiating, marketing, merchandising, social media, and networking, along with your experiential knowledge, the more both the consumer and you the agent, will become enveloped in a mutual celebration of your professional skill—and therefore influence.

There is a monumental difference between that which consumers appreciate from that which they value.

While homesellers may feel great fondness to a real estate agent for the professional and commendable way they kept in touch and kept them apprised of the transactional process (i.e. service), a million-dollar homeseller struggles in reconciling their appreciation over this service with having to pay (depending upon what the individual agent negotiated), in many cases, tens of thousands of dollars in payment for the service. Conversely, when a homeseller believes that their agent's skillful staging, marketing, and negotiating were responsible for receiving significantly more money than they could have achieved on their own, perceived value then becomes more commensurate with what homesellers believe they should be paying.

Presently, when real estate professionals and their companies ask consumers to rate their service versus their skills (CAR WASH), the respondents unavoidably are directed to lower value assessments. Assessments pertaining to follow-up, personal comportment, and results, as opposed to higher valued professional skills. How often have you heard colleagues lament, "Consumers think that I put the home on the MLS, stick a sign in the yard, sit at an open house, and then wait for the phone to ring." Yes, these are all services. Who is responsible for this woeful underrepresentation of your greater value? Could it be you?

Your greater value is in your skills.

Maximizing real estate influence also requires that there be a distinction between what constitutes service as opposed to services. Many agents who profess to provide 'great service' overlook the profound distinction between the service they personally provide and the real estate provided services they reflect and represent.

This lack of appreciation between the two often means the following. That regardless of whether an agent works for a brokerage that provides convenient one-stop-shopping services like mortgage, title, insurance, escrow, staging, moving, etc. or not, that this agent can still claim that they provide exceptional real estate service despite the absence of the agent's real estate ecosystem.

Exceptional personal service is not enough. Personal service must extend to relevant and timely services.

The situation is similar to how a doctor or nurse can provide 'great personal service' while, at the same time, not representing or providing convenient access to MRI machines, on-site labs, in-house pharmacy, and a host of other deeply appreciated services. Surveys reveal that consumers prefer one-stop shopping regarding their real estate transactions. Consider the difference between having a serious medical condition and visiting either an immediate or urgent care facility, a 'walk-in care', or a full-service hospital. If your medical need is basic, an excellent service like a 'walk-in' or smaller medical health-care facility might be sufficient. However, let's say that the employees at a facility are all wonderfully friendly and are supremely devoted to providing excellent service, but lack the array of services. This calls into question the value of their personal service.

The reason why I wanted to include a chapter regarding the relationship of service, services, and skills, and developing and sustaining influence, is most purposeful. If one approaches the 'Age of Real Estate Influence' only from the perspective of imitating the practices of the most iconic social media influences or determining which online platforms or offline methods of engagement in terms of their range, reach, and influence are most efficient, then I believe the real estate industry will never achieve an Age of True Real Estate Influence. True influence must evolve out of a higher intrinsic value, which is required to elicit true respect, indispensability, close the real estate loyalty gap, and to create a real estate ecosystem—not just because I am from Texas, but rather because it is an appropriate analogy.

I must say that optimizing influence requires a real estate Texas two-step. The two steps remind me of a quote attributed to the existential philosopher Goethe, "In order to do, you must first be." Step number one—you must first become more influential through the proper integration and separation of service, services, and skills. Step two—you now need to develop strategies—off and online, digitally, and face-to-face—to increase your range and reach after you have first prepared yourself to exponentially increase your clients and your ever-growing real estate ecosystem through significant elevated and self-discovered greater influence

In summary, personal service is just that...personal. Professional services must go well beyond your capabilities while also better refelecting your value. Professional skills is what, more than anything else, validates the highest level of your value.

Chapter 6—
Influencing Communities
Through Storytelling

The word 'community' is used to define many different groups or aspects of life that enjoy commonality. When you think of community, what is your most prominent association? One who is very social media-centric, might first consider their Facebook or other online communities. Many online communities provide a sense of fellowship where common attitudes, beliefs, concerns, and interests become socialized.

Communities can also refer to groups who organize based upon religion, ethnic affiliation, politics, country of origin, or love of animals. In this book, I discuss ecosystems which have been defined as a group of interdependent organisms of different species growing or living together in a specified habitat.

Yet, with all due respect to the plethora of the communities I've mentioned, along with the many more I haven't, I suggest that in many, if not most cases, the most important community for real estate professionals to influence would be the community of homeowners who reside within specifically branded neighborhoods, towns, or cities. This geographically based community can be described as a group of people residing within a commonly defined venue who also possess shared interests. What are the shared interests of most communities? Presumably, that their town or physical community be a clean and safe place to live. That where children are involved, that there be a proper school system. Often overlooked is the collective desire among all city or town homeowners that property values ascend versus descend within their municipal boundaries.

The significance of focusing on homeowner communities larger than what the real estate industry defines as 'geographical farm areas' is more important than ever. In order to preempt listing-side disruption, it is immeasurably more feasible to influence homesellers who are identifiably located within one geographical setting than it is to influence buyers who are monumentally more scattered. Buyers are less influenceable months and years before their transactional needs arise than are homesellers. Accordingly, this chapter is decidedly more dedicated to the need to influence physically identifiable homeowner communities existing in the form of neighborhoods, towns, and cities than any other community. This is not to say that other off and online aggregated communities are not deserving of your influence as well. I cover the importance of influencing online communities and real estate ecosystems in other chapters. The importance of forging relationships between real estate professionals and communities is not a new concept.

However, I believe there needs to be more attention devoted to the distinction between 'serving one's community', 'representing one's community', and 'representing the real estate interests of an entire town(s) or city. One definition of 'representing' is describing somebody or something. Congress-people go to Washington to tell the story that the voters in their district want narrated and, consequently, get re-elected over 95% of the time. To the contrary, real estate professionals tell their story to the community and get 're-elected' less than 20% of the time. This is because 'real estate representatives' represent communities and 'real estate professionals' only serve communities.

During my years at Intero Real Estate Services, and now as CEO of HSF Affiliates and Berkshire Hathaway HomeServices, I have witnessed innumerable real estate agents publicly extol how they serve their respective communities. The next time you come across a real estate agent's website, hosted bio, or read a professional brochure and learn that a particular agent is claiming or celebrating serving their community—I am sure it will neither be the first or last time you encounter this somewhat ubiquitous real estate related message.

This longstanding cliché, although reflecting a very important well-intentioned and certainly well-earned pronouncement of a real estate professional's life and career, does beg, at least for me, a most relevant and perhaps under asked question. Would citizens, consumers, and especially homeowners residing within such communities place greater value on the role of real estate professionals were they more dedicated to representing the home values of all town or city residents professionally versus the so-called conventional meaning of serving the community through volunteer work?

I believe that community residents would more greatly value real estate professionals who are equipped with comprehensive and well-honed marketing, social media, and selling skills, who additionally advocate persuasively on behalf of the entire town's real estate and lifestyle virtues. Although each area of volunteer service is important, appreciated, and certainly not in conflict with the objective of elevating all community home values, there is a significant difference between 'serving' and 'representing' the community.

Years ago, I asked an agent who was one of our top producers at Intero Real Estate Services, who featured in his Zillow posted bio how he had been serving the Morgan Hill community for over 25 years, to provide me with some particulars. To the best of my recollection, his response was somewhat expected. "Chris, I was a Pop Warner football coach for 15 years, I am a co-sponsor of our community blood drive, I helped raise money for our school's new soccer field, and I led a petition to prevent a cell tower from being built too close to one of our neighborhoods." I was impressed by the range and importance of all that my professional colleague and friend had contributed. Looking back, I remember reflecting upon my belief that more real estate agents are involved in serving their communities on a volunteer basis—arguably than any other vocational group. Serving one's community also, unquestionably, corresponds with gaining and sustaining personal and professional influence.

Consider the higher level of credibility and comfort generated when a referral is the result of working with fellow citizens in the collective pursuit of what is best for the community versus paying for a random lead.

There is indeed a so-called syllogistic benefit which exceeds one's altruistic motives when real estate agents serve their community.

For those unfamiliar with the meaning of syllogism, it refers to when logic and deductive reasoning lead to a logical conclusion.

Syllogisms were first used to achieve logical conclusions centuries ago:

> All people are mortal.
> All Greeks are people.
> All Greeks are mortal.

Now let's see how a syllogism relates to when real estate professionals do volunteer community work:

> I respect people who volunteer.
> This real estate agent volunteers.
> I respect this real estate agent.

This use of venerated logic is similar to when I speak at our Berkshire Hathaway HomeServices conventions regarding the Berkshire Hathaway HomeServices 'halo effect.' The halo effect means that if a company is good at one thing, then it most likely is good in all of its endeavors. When I speak in terms of creating a real estate ecosystem, I am also mindful of just how interwoven serving the community and creating this high-level network of influence operates.

With due respect to the concept of serving the community, I also, as mentioned earlier, believe an equal if not greater degree of sustainable influence can be acquired when instead of merely serving the community, one becomes known for representing the home values as a town or city advocate for the entire community. This higher level of targeted influence and elevated real estate-related relevance can only be achieved, in my view, when all homeowners, even those whom you do not represent, believe they are benefiting by virtue of your remarkable ability to elevate the perceived value of living in a community where their home resides.

Imagine what you would do if the city council or mayor of a particular town hired you to promote the benefits of living in that town. Since it is unlikely that any mayor, chamber of commerce or city council would select any individual agent to assume this task, why not appoint yourself to this position? One needs a signed agreement to represent an individual homeowner or builder, whereas no agreement is required to become that town or city's real estate town crier.

In other words, instead of listing homes why not list towns.

Here is my question for all who wish to exponentially elevate their influence within their local communities. If all of the homeowners in the town or city where you work were asked, "Which real estate agent in town does the best job of selling, marketing, promulgating, and overall promoting that particular town?"—what percentage of the

homeowners would emphatically point to you?
This will measure your Community IQ (Influence Quotient). This question is different from, who sells the most homes, who is the number 1 agent, who is the most professional, who is the number 1 real estate company, or when you think of real estate who first comes to mind.

I also believe that if you as an agent were asked, which two or three agents in your market sells the most homes, that your answer would probably be more forthcoming than if you were asked which two or three agents do the best job of selling or representing the real estate interests of the entire town, city, or community.

This ostensible lack of equal clarity surrounding who does the best job of selling and marketing homes versus marketing towns, cities, or states, is defensible and explicable. After all, you are not paid by the town for your results in marketing that community, nor by the county, state—or in Canada, the province—or in Europe, the region. And as mentioned, there does not exist an ethical or fiduciary responsible on your part to represent one town over another, as there is when representing one home over others. This client-related marketing differential means that even though, according to the National Association of Realtors®, that consumers overwhelmingly (approximately 75% of the time) are more willing to compromise on the home they select, the real estate industry collectively and overwhelmingly disproportionately directs its marketing, selling, and promotional skills towards elevating perceptions surrounding individual homes over towns, cities or neighborhoods.

The consequences of this offline and online digital marketing disparity, when it comes to marketing communities, is multifold.

A. Consumers, since they are not equally influenced through real estate agent narratives regarding the nuances and complexities of towns etc. delay engaging a real estate agent until after they first resolve which town, city, or neighborhood they are predisposed towards. This void represents a massively missed opportunity to insert professional influence earlier in the home search process.

B. The promotion of towns and cities—in lieu of the real estate industry doing more to refine community narratives—means that this task is instead assumed by the local chamber of commerce and tourism bureaus.
These town stakeholders, however, do not possess the ability commensurate with real estate professionals to comprehensively illuminate the many lifestyle virtues of the community extracted through the prism of years of learning from prospective buyers and homesellers what is valued most when living in that town.

C. Since the marketing of homes to many consumers appears to be somewhat commoditized, with every real estate company seemingly connected to MLS, IDX, Zillow, Realtor.com, and offering open houses, virtual tours, staging, and social media, the opportunity to distinguish oneself through the less crowded arena of marketing communities is not being opportunistically seized.

D. The marketing of homes has more to do with the aggregation of data and pictures, thereby inviting listing-side disruption, whereas the marketing of communities requires greater knowledge, wisdom, and context, which is best realized via the tenure and contextual community knowledge that is decidedly more the domain of real estate professionals than all others, including artificial intelligence.

E. I believe the entire real estate industry is in the middle of developing an almost narcissistic devotion to doing personal videos as part of our emerging storytelling society. Ask yourself this question:

What do you believe will give you greater influence in your community? Telling the community your story or telling the community story?

I believe that real estate agents rank amongst the most dedicated in volunteering to serve their communities. Real estate professionals are not alone however in their commitment to volunteering. Unquestionably, people of all backgrounds and motivations, both quietly and in some cases, with vivid visibility, also serve their communities. Although almost anybody associated with any particular community is both welcome and can find a way to serve a community, it cannot be said that just anybody can either assume or be accepted in the role of representing the entire home value interests of that community.

Regarding the representation or the act of advocating on behalf of an entire community of homeowners, I submit that no other profession is as well-suited for this representational role as are skillful real estate professional marke-teers. No other job or career comes to mind when looking for a natural connection and mutual interest in promoting the overall value of living within a community. Therefore, no other profession would be expected to focus on the goal of raising home equity. Town tax collectors and city tour-ism bureaus are not charged with this responsibility.

Simply put, tourism bureaus focus on tourists, tax collec-tors focus on taxes, just as the Chamber of Commerce is engaged in the limited focus of promoting a healthy mer-cantile environment.

Mayors, for their part, are unlikely to possess as deep a level of insight into the lifestyle nuances of each neighbor-hood. Even more disqualifying would be their lack of ex-periential knowledge pertaining to the lifestyle differences between numerous other competing towns or cities.

Consequently, one should not anticipate any time soon, attorneys, financial planners, so-called shopkeepers, or tradespeople announcing that they are producing a town or city video in order to extoll the overall lifestyle virtues of any particular community.

This is because dentists specialize in cavities, whereas real estate professionals are intimately connected to communities.

Even though all businesses and professions depend upon a healthy and thriving community for their business suc-cess and directly benefit from how the overall community is positively promoted as a great place to live, for them, this particular degree of holistic community-related marketing is neither their focus nor forte. How could these other community stakeholders possibly compete with the deep experiential knowledge that many (not all) real estate agents have acquired of each neighborhood, town or city from years of educating buyers regarding the vast and enriching lifestyle amenities and nuances which each community distinctively possesses?

In order to assume the de facto, non-fiduciary, real estate representation of communities and the home values of all of its residents, it might require the following refrain—that would be William H. Johnsen's notable saying, "If it is to be, it's up to me." Should the real estate industry, and specifically individual agents, seek to assume the role of promoting not only homes, which they do in an organized and comprehensive fashion, but also promote the town or city in which that property resides in a similar fashion? To do so will require combining marketing ethics with ethos. In most cases, depending upon real estate agency, real estate professionals assume an ethical responsibility to market their seller client's home to the fullest. Maximizing the marketing of a home also includes lifestyle and community-related information as it pertains to the subject property's overall value. This duty is often described along ethical terms because the homeowner and their agent are ethically 'to become one' in terms of seeking the best possible outcome. Conversely, real estate professionals do not possess an ethical responsibility to represent the collective real estate interest of the entire community.

Accordingly, real estate professionals are not expected to assume or work towards elevating all home values. This is where the concept of ethos enters into the marketing equation. Ethics relates to what you must do. Ethos, in addition to what you have to do, concerns itself with what you should do. As the only professionals either living in and/or serving the community who can also best represent the home values of the entire community, this might mean that you also consider this task as part of your real estate ethos. Again, "If it is to be (the promotion of the entire community), it must be me." On the other hand, your real estate ethos might be, "I don't want to contribute to all home values being elevated because I do not want either my buyer, or buyers in general, to have to pay more."

It is up to you to decide whether you want to have influence beyond transactions and whether or not to use your marketing talent to pre-sell the towns or communities in which you work.

By demonstrating an ability to skillfully narrate the past, present, and future value of communities, where properties reside, and where agents market homes, this will go a long way to validate the ever-growing proclamation, "I don't just sell homes, I sell lifestyles." Without displaying an equal ability to capture the essence of each community, off and online, with the same level of comprehensiveness as marketed homes receive, this aforementioned statement comes across as a tired, overused, hollow, and hackneyed cliché. The way to exponentially increase your influence within the communities you seek to represent, to become top of mind, and become the talk of the town, is "to talk about that town". There are many ways to accomplish this objective, both off and online. Social media, advertisements, direct mail, brochures, billboards, park benches, shopping carts, videos, etc., can all serve as vehicles conveying your passionate advocacy for the city or towns that you positively position.

I believe the most influential method of advocating for any community would be through the production of a world-class video.

Producing a video, which compellingly conveys and captures the highlights which contribute to the irresistibility of certain communities for segments of buyers, when done properly, can "stratospherically" increase your influence.

The community video production process requires debunking a myth:
Specifically, that in order for a video to be effective, its duration should not exceed, in some cases 90 seconds—and almost all others be no longer than 2 minutes.

While Google metrics support these assumptions, based upon documented drop off rates, these findings do not pertain to the development of a wide variety of specialty video offerings, and especially community videos.

To make my point, please consider Ted Talks. The iconic Ted Talks, noted for the success of their legendary videos, present their video offering with an average length of 17 to 20 minutes. Have you ever wondered why millions of people happily absorb the entire length of these videos?

It is because the audience is interested in the subject matter, and the content is very well presented. Additionally, observers anticipate a comprehensive and up to 20-minute video experience. If you were going to pay for the wedding video of a family member, would you capitulate to Google's recommendation that the video should be kept to under 90 seconds? Why not? Because when serious subjects are introduced to where there is serious interest, one or two minutes is far too limiting. Moreover, severe abbreviation in many cases can actually be harmful or counterproductive if one senses information is being held back or there is not sufficient value to warrant more time. There are tens of thousands of towns in North America that I wouldn't take 2 minutes of my time to explore through a video narrative. I also cannot imagine many of us taking more than a minute or two, if any time at all, to watch wedding videos of strangers, just as I recognize that certain friends of mine would not take 20 minutes to watch a Ted Talk on how to create a compelling corporate culture, even if they were paid to watch. If anyone in the real estate industry believes they can satisfactorily provide even adequate 'sizzle' pertaining to the complexity surrounding cities, towns, counties, states, and provinces, in 90 to 120 seconds, resulting in buyers or corporations developing a deep interest in moving there—if you'll forgive me—good luck.

To the contrary, when individuals and families are trying to discern and decide which town amongst several, which school systems, which services, which levels of safety, which houses of worship, recreational offerings, ecological footprint, cultural offerings, shopping opportunities, trending values, etc. to select, their relationship to the length of the video experience significantly changes. Consumers are more than willing to take more than 2 minutes to experience a community video, considering the innumerable hours spent online, and days driving through the community, to become more illuminated regarding this epic and life transformative decision.

I also believe that prospective homesellers, in addition to countless community residents, will be intrigued to discover how their town is being portrayed to those considering moving there and its relationship to their home's value. Homeowners who realize that not only does their home compete with other homes, but their town is in competition with other towns, and who are curious as to the marketing ability of their prospective agent, unquestionably will take the requisite several minutes to determine whether the merits of their community is being appropriately captured and conveyed. Therefore, I suggest that in order to do a world-class video on your community, you should be prepared to produce visual and textual content that will run in the range of 5 to 10 minutes.

Now that we have covered length, lets now examine the relationship between creating the right blend of images, script, narration, and music. My research has led me to believe that the narrative, or overall storytelling of a town or city, is the most important component of a community video, even more important than the visuals.

This is a case where the right words are worth a thousand pictures—versus one picture being worth a thousand words.

Countless towns, relatively speaking, feature indistinguishable hills, rivers, seashores, waves, mountains, train stations, boutiques, restaurants, parks, schools, skies, sunsets, and snow. Watching a video of Colorado's mountains, California's beaches, or Cape Cod's quaint harbors, while pleasant to view, does not change in the slightest, anything I already imaged about these venues. In almost all cases, if a prospective buyer was not already aware of these most celebrated and most representative amenities, they wouldn't even be considering a move to that region. Therefore, what is required is more hyper-local and nuanced context and narrative, which provides deeper interest and value being placed upon a particular local city, town, and neighborhood. For many, if not most, the greater curiosity is satisfied through experiencing a narration that masterfully addresses dozens of requisite lifestyle touchpoints that speak to a far broader range of interests and daily life needs for the individual and/or family.

To many parents, the image of a school building unsurprisingly is not as remarkable as the range of academic metrics. A deeper presentation of major lifestyle considerations must be superbly articulated and interwoven with arresting images. The singular importance of words, experienced by many, can be found in the following example: How often, after reading a book—and subsequently viewing a movie based upon the book—have you thought that you liked the book much better? This common conclusion is because nothing exceeds the images one attaches to evocative words.

Obviously, a powerful video must integrate both magnificent words and images, yet there is a reason why I am disproportionately stressing the importance of the words. We must remember that we live in a world where almost anybody with a handheld device, or paying for a drone, can capture images. The development of a relevant and resonant description of the overall allure of a community cannot be performed with corresponding ease. One must almost forensically slave over each and every word in order to convince homesellers that you, the 'real estate professional storyteller,' can serve as the deserved steward of the unique legacy and promise of that respective community. An additional incentive behind my passionate plea that you rigorously consider how you characterize communities within your video production is based upon my knowledge that the real estate industry essentially uses only five words to describe all homes and two cliches to capture the essence of all landscaping.

Community videos must reach beyond homes being described as beautiful, charming, gracious, spacious, or elegant and extend our definition of landscaping beyond the ubiquitous use of 'professionally landscaped' and 'park-like setting.'

When you produce a professional community video, your influence within your community will soar, provided you do the following:

1. Promote off and online directly to the community the following message: "Before you buy or sell a home, you must see this video."

2. Promote the community video as part of your pre-marketing/listing packet with the following message; "Before we discuss the marketing of your home, I thought you might like to see how I market your town."

3. Have links on your website to your community videos. Make sure that in no video do you proclaim that any one town is the best place to live. Instead, have each video for different reasons, bring out the very best in every town. You want homeowners in all towns not to think that you have a favorite town, but instead, when representing their home, you also possess the ability to do a better job of including their town as a part of the overall lifestyle decision.

4. When asked by homesellers who will see this video about our town, consider saying this: "Every serious buyer or buyer agent who has interest in your property will be provided a link to this video."

5. Consider showcasing the video on a loop at your open houses as a great way to receive email addresses.

6. Show the video at real estate events where the community is invited.

The ultimate motivation for including this chapter, one which Allan Dalton and I specifically collaborated on and one which explores influencing homeowners within their communities, is not to narrowly define community influence as a result of creating community videos. Rather it is to call attention to the need for a greater level of advocacy on behalf of towns and cities, whether this objective takes the form of community seminars, overall community event marketing, community newsletters, or the strategic use of online content or targeted and hyper-local geo-targeted mobile in-app marketing.

Whatever the medium one selects, the emphasis must be on creating and delivering content that illuminates as many reasons as possible for selecting particular neighborhoods, towns, and cities in which to live. I will leave it to you to unleash your marketing acumen, creativity, and compelling communication to accomplish the objective of not only serving your communities but also representing and exponentially influencing them.

For those of you who might have expected a list of civic organizations or a focus on community gatherings, volunteer work within the community or becoming the 'man or woman about town,' all of those ideas come under the auspices of serving. Many of those activities, I would hope you might participate in even if there wasn't a presumed real estate payoff. Allan and I wanted, instead, to focus exclusively on the immense influence that can be derived when you, above all others, excel at representing the real estate values of the entire community in the same way that a sales and marketing manager does for a development— no one is going to offer you the job of the marketing director for any town or city, you must claim it through your marketing, your value, which will create incomparable influence.

Any discussion regarding influencing communities would be significantly incomplete without my emphatically reminding all readers to the importance of diversity and inclusion.

One of the reasons why Allan and I asked Charlie Oppler, the President of the National Association of Reatlors, to write the foreword for *Real Estate Influence* was when we observed the unprecedented attention he is devoting toward the importance of Fair Housing.

There is clearly a nexus between Fair Housing, diversity and inclusion.

Yet, as I often hear from Teresa Palacios Smith, the former President of The National Association of Hispanic Real Estate Professionals (NAHREP), legendary leader of diversity and inclusion, and founder of Women Who Lead, say, "Diversity and inclusion vigilance is not only the moral way to do business but also the most profitable way to do business."

That said, the fact that diversity and inclusion is the moral path to business should transcend any and all other considerations. I therefore wish to also acknowledge the following organizations—Asian Real Estate Association of America (AREAA), National Association of Hispanic Real Estate Professionals (NAHREP), National Association of Real Estate Brokers (NAREB), LGBTQ+ Real Estate Alliance, Veterans Association of Real Estate Professionals (VAREP), and Women in the Housing and Real Estate Ecosystem (NAWRB), Professional Women in Building (PWB), and Women's Council of REALTORS® (WCR).

Chapter 7—
An Interview with Author,
Neal Schaffer

The most basic understanding of influence cannot be achieved without acknowledging that one must be open to receiving influence in order to promulgate influence. My work on the subject of real estate influence reflects the significant influence I have experienced from Allan Dalton. My work on the The Real Estate IQ System lead me to also bring accomplished author on the subject of influence, Neal Schaffer, onto my team.

Neal is the author of the critically acclaimed book, *The Age of Influence*. Real estate influence can't and does not operate in its own environment apart from overall societal and business influence—in fact, real estate influence should be viewed as a tributary and part of a larger influential ecosystem connected to an ocean of influence.

This chapter is an unedited transcription of an interview I conducted with Neal as part of my *Forever Agent Podcast* series. I am sure you find it most illuminating.

STUART

Neal, let's jump right in. First of all, thank you for your time and being a part of this book with us. I'm really very excited about it.

SCHAFFER

I'm honored, Chris.

STUART

Neal, in your opinion, what impact has the internet and specifically social media had on the opportunities for individuals to be influential?

SCHAFFER

Chris, the internet and social media has democratized the flow of information, the publication of information and, the influence of information. What I mean by this is—if you were an agent or a broker 30 years ago, to get the word out about your business, the channels were so few and far between, and they were costly. Now anyone can set up a social media profile for free and become a publisher, contribute to the internet, potentially have their information be seen, and have their advice followed. It's made it much easier for individuals and businesses to become influential because more and more people, instead of reading the newspaper and watching TV, are now on social media and doing internet searches. Therefore, we all have an equal opportunity to influence people.

Chris, I have a new case study to share based on my use of Twitter. A few years ago I had sent out a tweet when some friends of mine were evacuated from Fukushima when the tsunami hit Japan. The next morning I had a direct message from a BBC reporter who wanted to interview that family. More recently, California had devistating brush fires. The fire in Orange County was called "The Bonfire." I was following that term as a hashtag and a reporter on Twitter shared that they were looking to interview people experiencing the fire. So, I tweeted out. I sent a photo of the smoke and shared my experience over

Twitter. A few hours later, I got a message from a reporter from the Associated Press. This all happened last week!

Chris, this is just an example. This is not influence. This is not an area that I want to be influential in but imagine if I was tweeting, blogging, and posting information about something I was an expert in or something I did for my business. When someone is looking for an answer, they can find me, they follow me, and at some point they can follow my advice. If they can reach out for advice, they become a customer. That's how being active on social media and the internet, with content publication over blogs, podcasts, and YouTube videos, can get you found and you can become more influential over time for whatever you talk about. That's the key thing. If I was to talk politics all day, I'm going to become an influencer for politics. If I'm talking about my community all day, I'll be seen as an expert influencer in that community, and therefore over time, people will tend to listen to me and come to me for advice.

STUART

You mentioned a buzzword hot topic there. A potentially hot potato topic—that of politics—and someone once said that any publicity is good publicity. I think about some of our agents, not necessarily just in our network, but in the industry ranting about politics, taking a position one way or the other, and that sometimes generates some pretty bad publicity for them. As to the statement, "Any publicity is good publicity." Do you agree or has the role of technology and visibility through social media changed that at all?

You hit on a good point. I think that because of the way that social media works, it amplifies the good and the bad. Amplifying the good is great, but when the bad is amplified, it can have extremely negative consequences for people. We all feel pulled into talking about politics. I think, more than ever, recent events have made more and more people want to make a stand, and I believe for younger generations, especially.

Everybody must remember that their information is public and people whom you may have never imagined could see that information may do so–for good or bad. So, the positive is that you attract similar-minded people, and you may gain even more passionate fans who believe in the same things you believe in. On the other hand, you're turning away half the country when you do that. So, it's really tricky. Generally, I would say just stay away, but I know with recent events, it's going to be harder and harder for people to do so. Obviously, you should always keep your deepest opinions offline. You simply never know when they could be used out of context. We see comments made by politicians being taken out of context all the time, and we don't want that to happen to agents. On Facebook, there are ways of sharing things to a just few people. You can create a friends list and only share certain information or oppinion with them. If you truly feel you need to get something off your chest on Facebook, that is the approach I would take.

STUART

Excellent advice. What are two or three other effective social media strategies you see as being the anchors for much of your teachings and working with your clients?

SCHAFFER

I'd say the most important thing is, which I hinted at in the beginning, "You are what you tweet." If you want to yield more influence in a certain topic, you need to talk about that topic. This gets down to the role of content in the social media experience for anyone that wants to become more influential. Knowing the end game of your content is key. What are you trying to achieve with your influence? As an agent, if you're trying to achieve business in your hometown, understanding the target market and the target audience—Marketing 101—, must shape that content so that it is attractive to that target audience. At times, this is something a lot of people who want to be more influential online forget about. If you want to focus on particular communities, particular lifestyles, you should be talking about that. If you're always talking about saving money at Target, what have you, you're going to attract a certain demographic versus if you are talking about the top 10 ski resorts in Vail. It's not just having content that's focused but content taht is really aligned with your target audience to better reach your goals. The third part, I'd say, is really about branding, about "who you are" online. That profile photo, that description of you, they all must be aligned with what you do for a living and what it is you want to become influential on. People sometimes forget this. I think anybody that looks at a LinkedIn, Instagram, or Twitter profile—and we have analytics for these platforms—we can see how many people come to our profile and how many people take action.

There are a lot of people that come to peoples' profiles that are not following them, that are not engaging with them. They are lurkers and they make up to 90% of users. You want to make sure that, for these users, your branding is set up in a way that "paints the best picture of you." If I was to add a fourth tip, I'd say collaboration. You find a lot of influencers in various industries collaborate with each other. This is a really powerful tactic for people who want to yield more from their relationships. There's a lot of credibility and social proof for your influence when you're able to show yourself engaging and collaborating with other influencers in your community or in your market.

There are a lot of different ways to collaborate. Collaborating—or cross-pollinating if I may use an agricultural term—through content or Facebook Live with each other's audiences is a really powerful way of growing influence. "Standing on the shoulders of other influencers." This is something I challenge agents with when we talk about sphere of influence. When I talk to brands, I talk about their customers. When we talk to agents, we talk about their customers as well, but there are also ecosystem partners that they may have. Really finding those key influencers and ways to collaborate with them, to really raise the bar for everyone involved, is something I'd like to see more agents practically do.

STUART

Great insight. To explore that topic even further, it's obvious that traditional marketers have attempted to segment their audiences on the basis of demographics, geographies, and psycho-graphics—and a range of other attributes. I'm curious, in your opinion, is that the right approach? Should real estate professional also be aware of these attributes within their markets and appeal to them differently? Or should they remain more consistent and authentic, even while remaining connected to a wide variety of different people within their ecosystem?

SCHAFFER

So, we have this concept in the marketing of targeted personas, even in social media marketing people talk about avatars. What is the perfect avatar? The challenge is that there is no one perfect avatar. You cannot say your customers are only going to be 28 years old, or 48 years old. It's obviously going to be a range of people, and it's going to be dependent upon so many factors. I think understanding, in general, that target demographic is very important, but once you get out there online on social media, it's not like the old days where the information flow is very limited. You're going to attract a broad range of people and some of these people are going to engage with you more than others. For some, your message is going to resonate with them more than others, and some of them are going to tend to become your customers more than others.

I think a more modern approach is, as you build this community of influence, the art of serving them, of getting to know more about them. Why are they interested in you? What are their real estate needs? You find a lot of marketers these days talk more about trying to align your message, not with a fictional target persona, but with the actual audience that is engaging with you, that respond to you, that will complete a survey, so that you better how to talk the way they talk, how to position your content with the way they consume content. I think that's just a general best practice. You need to start somewhere with these attributes. I find a lot of marketers spend way too much time getting lost in the weeds. I would rather like to see them out there starting to engage, seeing who comes along for the ride, and getting to know those people better. Why did they come along for the ride? What are their needs? How can you best serve them and obviously making customers out of them?

STUART

Is it fair to say that in the absence of content, influence is completely unattainable? In other words, does content precede influence?

SCHAFFER

Offline influence is a whole other story. There are influential CEOs that don't even show up on social media, but they still have incredible influence in the business world. Regarding online influence, the whole idea about social media, if we define it, is that you have a user profile and user-generated content published that profile. Content is the way people learn to know and trust you. Once they find you and see your content, they get to know you, and over time with consistency, begin to trust you. Content is the currency of social and digital media.

When thinking about the format of content, what is your priority in working with your customers—specifically in terms of the sequence surrounding the format of the content? When you work with your clients, do you customize a content chronology with them?

This is the next book I am still in the process of conceptualizing, Chris, but that's the playbook that I want to create. We have always been digital-first as consumers, but due to the pandemic, it has taken businesses more time to play catch up. Those companies which were more digital or transformed their sales and marketing digitally were more accelerated, obviously, and I believe did better than those that are still trying to play catch up. When we think digital-first, what are people doing online digitally? Well, they're either searching for information, on social media, or they're in their inboxes slash reading texts. So, if you think about it that way, it comes down to search, social, email.

The most important thing to remember is that you need to have a gateway. You need to have a digital gateway for your company, and the best digital gateway, obviously, is a website, and if you have a website, you want it to become discovered. The best way to get your website discovered is through content published on that site, which leads to it being indexed in search engines, which leads to traffic. So, I believe the beginning is the website...content in the form of blog content, because the lifetime of a social media post is very short. Now, you do see some blog content continue to get traffic year, after year, after year. In fact, if you were to do a search for something on Google, often the results come from content that's a year old, two years old, sometimes even five or 10 years old. So, with that in mind, and just the number of the volume of searches being done obviously is huge. Therefore, I double down on content and I begin with the website.

Now, above and beyond the website, that's where you get into podcasts, which are audio, you have a video for YouTube, and then you have the social media. So, after your website, if you want to tap into the podcast or the YouTube, I consider those only after you're pretty confident, you have a good game plan, and you're already implementing and finding really good success with your web content. On the other hand, going into 2021, it's very, hard to compete because there are so many companies trying to rank for keywords. It requires a lot of money, money for content, money for SEO, and you're competing against big companies. If you are a big company, great. But if you're an agent and a blogger, I say, "Let corporate aid in ranking those keywords."

If you want to rank for community keywords, local keywords. That's another story. That's the role where local brokers and agents succeed. Again, getting high ranking for keywords on Google is very competitive. You need to have that content there anyway, but this is where we begin to look at YouTube and podcasts because there aren't as many publishers on YouTube or on podcasts and very, very few companies. As the playing field is far more level, it will be easier for you to cut through the noise and be heard and discovered. I believe that today, YouTube or a podcast, will get you discovered more than a blog.

So that's really the search part, right? After we do the search part, I move on to email. The reason for that is that, when people come to your website, you want to move them, get them to interact. What do you want them to do? Do you want them to contact you? Well, some people might contact you. Most people leave. How do we develop a relationship with them? That relationship can be done through email, through providing them something of value, which we call a lead magnet. It could be a 10% off coupon. It could be a free e-book you've already created. We are seeking to acquire their email address to keep the conversation going —daily, weekly, monthly. We want to continue to have communication with them. You want to begin to have a funnel. The way I talk about it in my new book is creating "a funnel of relationships."

You start out with nothing, you have a digital gateway, you want to be discovered by search engines. Once people come to your website, you want to bring them further down into your funnel and email is the next logical step— unless they contact you. If you don't have that in place, and you go to social media first, they're probably going to click on a link to your website, and what are they going to find? Are they going to find the content they're looking for? Are they going to find something that's going to opt them in to your email list to continue that communication? This is why, for me, the last step is social. Why this funnel of relationships works is really, really easy to see because when you start a profile, and nobody follows you, you're a single entity in a sea of billions of social media users. Sure, you can begin attracting the general public but when you begin to followers, when you begin to bring people into your sphere of influence digitally, that's when the process is working. People now have the ability to find your content every day, instead of just when they do a search on Google. Once people become our followers, part of our engagers sphere, or a ring in the funnel, is when all these content components are working together.

Chris, I treat every engagement like a Japanese tea ceremony. The idea is that every single unique engagement is a unique opportunity to deepen that relationship and drive people further down into the funnel. "Going further down" means becoming part of your email list, becoming a customer, becoming a fan, becoming an advocate who is going to talk about you and spread word of mouth about you. That's really the core of influential marketing.

Search, email, social, they all have their roles, but I think when you look at it strategically, you begin to see where the pieces fall into place. A lot of people tend to gravitate towards YouTube videos and podcasts. I tell people to stay with the basics until you feel you're doing really well, then branch out. Unfortunately, social media content doesn't go that far, but the relationships can go really far. What I'm saying, Chris, is thst I think businesses and agencies need to focus more on the one-to-one than the traditional one-to-many. The one-to-one of the email relationship, the one-to-one of the follower relationship, and then of the advocacy relationship. That's where you're going to get the biggest bang for your buck in 2021, and beyond I believe.

STUART

What a great response—and so key. Adding onto another comment you made earlier—which is the role of collaborating and cross-pollinating with other folks in your ecosystem—can you speak to how you've seen people watch other influencers and achieve this collaboration dynamic that you spoke about? How do I choose the influencers that I'm listening to? What should I be observing? And what are some best practices or things that you've seen work in terms of really leveraging that?

SCHAFFER

I'm not a big fan of kissing up to influencers to be recognized by them. Ten years ago, I began blogging about fifteen to twenty of the best social media books by my favorite authors. Organically, I began getting comments from some of those authors—people like Guy Kawasaki and Mari Smith. Thanks to this, I was able to develop relationships with them soley because I mentioned them in a blog post. This is a great way to begin to develop influence. That can translate into collaboration. Using the analogy of writing a blog or social media post, if you were to tag businesses you wanted to build a relationship with, say, the top five house painters in Irvine, California. You would assume they all have profiles and can now connect to on your account. If Instagram is your social platform of choice, maybe you're targeting a younger audience. We're talking about sphere of influence here. You could be seeking to connect with lawyers, banks, what have you. Look for industries where people are active on Instagram. If they have a greater following than you do, create a post that says, "Hey, these are the five painters that I recommend to all my clients. Are your favorites here?" You can guess what will happen when you do this. Let's say you just pick five painters on Instagram. Number one, they're all going to thank you, right? So, you're going to deepen your relationship with them by mentioning them. If you don't have a relationship with them, this is going to begin that relationship. You can now connect with them by saying, "Hey, if you're ever looking to collaborate, and there are a lot of ways we can collaborate, let me know. Maybe you have a discount for clients I send your way?" That's one possible interaction. Another thing that might happen is that all the other painters who saw your post—for whatever reason, maybe because of a hashtag—and weren't included on the list now will want become your best friend. "Hey, why don't you include me? Hey, what can I do? Hey, you know what, I'm so committed to my work that the next time you have a client that needs a room painted, I'm going to paint a room for free" Even today I continue write these types of blog posts, recommending marketing tools, and I do it as a service to my community. In return, every day, I get another company saying, "Hey, I noticed you mentioned all these other tools. Why didn't you mention my company's tool?" In return they'll say, "Hey, we'll give you free lifetime use our tool." You're not trying to influence these business for little fringe benefits, but when you start publishing content about things, tagging people, and talking about people, it's going to attract both outcomes. Or you could say, "Hey, this is my network. Before we sell a home, this is the group of five people that I'm always in touch with. I'd like to introduce them to you." So you're appreciating your network, you're promoting them, you're looking for deeper ways to collaborate, and then those other people are going to reach out saying, "Hey, next time if your stager is busy, I do staging as well. Let me get to know you."

STUART

Neal, I often talk about the triumvirate of know, like, and trust. I'm just curious as to your opinion as to the difference between being known and being influential.

SCHAFFER

You can't yield influence until you're known. So, I think being known is the first step in becoming influenial. Now they know you and there is a sense of trust. They also sense credibility, trustworthiness, and, in some instances, authority. You are now someone that they can reach out to and have a conversation with, knowing that you're on a similar wavelength and they can trust their business with you. Chris, everything I talked about here, content, the whole role of the content, all of this is to help you get known. An imporatnt thing to remember is you can't simply stop at getting known. You will never yield as much influence if you don't continue building the content, the branding. This will lead to disengagement.

STUART

So, being known is all about the short game, being influential is the long game. Is that a fair description?

SCHAFFER

Correct. Once you yield influence you need to make sure you maintain that influence. My son made the Development Academy soccer team a few years ago, whe was 11 or 12. The first thing his coach said, "Congratulations, but just know that a year from now, everyone wants your spot." If you are not using influence once you yeild some, others are going to try to steal the spotlight from you because there are only so many people we can follow, so many people that we can consider in our trusted network of advisors. That's the final concept, that's the ultimate long game—be known, gain influence, and then really leveraging that influence.

STUART

Agreed. For certain salespeople, and maybe marketers as well, there's always this fine line between influencing and advising, guiding and manipulating. In your opinion, based on your experience and observations across industries, where do you see that line between wielding influence and manipulating?

SCHAFFER

The bottom line is, Chris, you need to serve others. There's a quote from a senior VP at Walmart that I used in my presentations right after the pandemic started. "Businesses exist to serve society." As long as you are serving society and serving your community, you are not manipulating them, you're being helpful. When you stop serving the community because you want to serve yourself, that's where I think actions fall more into manipulation—that you would do anything so that you can get ahead instead of allowing your community to advance. Continuing to serve others and the community, to me, is the guiding light. No matter if it seems too optimistic or simplistic of a perspective.

It's kind of the golden rule. It's about a switch to selfless from selfish. Also, ultimately, are you advising on the basis of what's in the best interest of the other person, which is selfless, and are you advising on the basis of things that you do yourself?

Absolutely. I've been in some interesting real estate transactions where I wonder if the agent was really trying to serve his or her community or try to increase the probability that they're going to get a commission check earlier rather than later. You may not know this but I actually went to real estate school. I never got licensed, but I went to the school to get licensed three or four years ago. There they discussed the importance of agency, the meaning of agent, what you represent. You're not an entrepreneur, you're representing the buyer or the seller in their transaction. As an agent, your role is to serve others. As long as you stick to that and you remind yourself this is the job you are meant to do, like Steve Jobs was known to do every day in the mirror, then you will succeed. You are there to serve others and when you serve others and make them happy, good things come your way. Trust the process and it will happen.

Neal, switching gears now towards the company perspective of influence, can you give our audience some examples of companies that in your opinion have done a great job of influencing or being influential?

116

Wow. Big consumer brands have always been influential. They're always in the center of things. One great way I believe Dunkin' Donuts did recently was that they partnered with Charli D'Amelio, a teenaged TikTok star. They created a drink for her which then promoted on TikTok and social media. This is a great example of product collaboration. Take Air Jordans of the past. Collaborating with influencers obviously helps brands like Dunkin' Donuts expose their products to their current audience but also aligns them with new ones. If young people have been going to Starbucks and see Dunkin' Donuts aligned with Charli D'Amerlio, it inspires them to think, "Hey, Dunkin' Donuts is cool." It's a celebrity endorsement, right? "So-and-so is drinking their stuff; so should you."

Ocean Spray cranberry juice similarly collaborated with someone on TikTok, where the person was drinking their product on a skateboard. In doing so, Ocean Spray aligned with an up-and-coming influencer and platform to built a lot of goodwill. Many brands are becoming very smart in this way now. They realize that if their social media reach declining, they can reverse that and become more influential by collaborating with people in different ways. A case study I enjoy sharing in presentations that of a company called Rosefield, a European watch company based out of Amsterdam. Recently, they have essentially created a community, an army of influencers, and major visibility on social media. They did this by going into their email database, their social media followers lists, and their customer database to analyize these people's influence in social media. We call these people "nano-influencers," people with like a thousand followers. The tactic is to reach out to people who might not know your brand well, offer get to know them, and encourage them to collaborate. Also, you can focus on working with people you already like, know, and trust, and in doing so, establish them as an open and inclusive brand ambassador-community that gains exclusivity to newly released products before anye else and store credit points. There's no exchange of money. The brand gets incredible benefits, and the people that are part of it—their customers—equally benefit.

When brands and companies recognize people and bring them in, amazing things happen. Just another case study, my business banks with Bank of America. A few weeks ago, I got an email that I was invited to a Bank of America advisory panel for small businesses. You think, "Wow, Bank of America chose me!" It makes you feel happy. You feel more aligned, and it builds a deeper relationship with the brand. Unfortunately, when I entered this "advisory committee," all they were doing was handing out a bunch of survey questions. I got no value out of it, and I immediately left. So there's a good way to do this and a bad way to do this. Chris, earlier in my career I had a job offer at Proctor and Gamble to do product marketing for their Bounce product in Japan. I turned down that offer, but what I realized was that these big brands, unlike in the old days before social media, wanted to create distance between themselves and the consumer. In doing so, they were essentially saying, "We are the brand. We dictate things. We create cool things. We create entertaining TV commercials." There was distance. Now, due to social media, and how it effects each generation, brands have realizes that the closer they get to the consumer, the better it's going to be for everybody. It makes them more relatable, more authentic, and it builds a deeper relationship than the old paradigm of, "We want to be far apart from people. People can't contact us or tweet at us." If we remember the funnel of relationships I talked about, the closer you can get to your customers, the more they will have interest in your business. That's where you get the biggest bang for your marketing buck. Influencer marketing is about tapping into your internal and external influencers who already like, know and trust you, rather than trying to align with people that just have a lot of followers.

STUART

That makes a lot of sense, Neal. So, I would deduce that consumers are more effectively influenced by people than by companies. Is that a fair statement?

SCHAFFER

Absolutely. Social media was made for people, not for businesses. I say this a lot. YouTube, podcasts, ecetera are dominated by people, right? When we do a search on Google, we tend to see company results. Companies could have become YouTubers; they could have become Instagrammers and TikTokers. They have the money, they have the assets, they have the people to do it, but they didn't, right? Now did they try? I don't know, but yes, we resonate with people that are like us. In the old days, the only thing we saw on video screens were TV and movie stars in ads. Now we see our friends. We see people. Today when we see brand advertisements that aren't authentic, they almost looks out of place. If we had a neuropsychologist here, he or she would say that obviously, we resonate with people's photos more than with brand logos. We resonate more with actual words that sound like something we may say than with marketing speak coming out of businesses.

STUART

Well said, Neal, and so relative to the journey of establishing likability, trust and influence as a real estate professional—versus what you see amongst influencers in other industries. How do you imagine that journey? If someone were to be starting from—not from scratch because I don't think any of us are at a point zero in terms of our existing social networks—but how do you imagine that that maturation process amongst real estate professionals?

SCHAFFER

I'd like to keep it as simple as possible. Most agents that I've met are extremely social. They're good at conversation. They know a lot of information about my community and obviously about real estate, and some of them are generally really, really interesting, entertaining people. Some of the best out there. That said, why do agents find it difficult to translate those talents online? If they were to translate those offline skills online, I think they will, number one, make a lot more friends, number two, be able to share information which will help them become more influential and, number three, I believe it will lead to a broadening of people who will now like, know, and trust them.

When one looks to reset their social media presence, they need to do so with the understanding their goal is now to serve a broader community, which will include potential buyers. It is important to strategically think about the content being posted if you are going to effectively create a deeper connection with the community. A few years back, I lived in a community near Irvine where a Realtor parked a van with their name on it, right outside of the elementary school. It was parked in such a way that everyone had to pass by it twice a day. Once when they dropped their kids off and once when they picked them up. I think of publishing on social media and commenting on other people's posts as something very similar.

You want to be seen and you want to be seen talking about things that are going to resonate with your community, which often is about the community, right? The new restaurant that opened up, or the new ballet school, I don't know, there's obviously a lot of things that you can talk about. But not just staying out there to become that van people pass by. This time it's not physically, but virtually in a feed in social media. You have to not only be proactive to show up in other people's feeds, you comment on what you have to offer the community. It may be a few-step processes, but re-sinking your strategic objective with your content and your branding is important. Once that has taken place, it's really imporant to create more of these collaborations and partnerships with people in your community that will drive your efforts even further.

STUART

Neal, this has been so insightful and directing in terms of some of these best practices. Thank you so much for your willingness to share. Just a couple of final questions. The first would be—what do you believe are some of the most critical activities or areas of focus for establishing influence offline so that there's some symmetry between what's happening in an agent's business online? What are your thoughts there?

SCHAFFER

If yielding influence online is all about showing up and being out there, I think the same goes for offline. Community events, it's being there. When that new restaurant opens up, you're in line along with everybody else. Once again, think of your target market, your target audience, where would they be if they wanted to experience the best of where you live in terms of offline activities. Whether you know anyone there or not, the wonderful result is what we call O2O, online to offline. When you have an online relationship, and then you meet someone in this virtual relationship physically, it only brings that relationship forward two, three, four times. I remember walking into Legoland with my family a few years ago and someone came up to me and said, "Are you Neal Schaffer? I read your book. I follow you online." It may have been a simple interaction, but now I remember who that person is, and it obviously helped our relationship to become that much deeper because of it.

STUART

So, in a similar way, if you are able to see people that follow you, that you know from being active in the community, when you join these events or when you show up offline, that's great. But even if not, the content and photos you take in the moment are going to be great for you online. Either way, you're going to get the benefit of doing it, but yeah, you need to be active. And I think agents, in general, are probably more successful at the offline, the chamber of commerce meetings, the breakfast lunch and learns, the community events.

I think of other things that can produce the same effect. Maybe aligning themselves with schools, for instance. I was on the PTA committee for my son's elementary school. These are really easy ways to build more influence in your community. I was aldo on the marketing committee for the United Way of Orange County for a year, where I got to engage with other business leaders from my community. Align yourself with nonprofits or schools. If your kids are in school, that's really easy, but a nonprofit is a wonderful way to really get invested in your community. It gives you the excuse to show up more offline. And, obviously, you want to do it because you want to serve, you're not doing this to leverage it for influence. As a by-product, it does help you be seen by more people and offers you more interesting things to talk about in your social media feeds. So, if you think you're running out of ideas, all these experiences will give you a lot of good things to share and attract the right people with.

Wonderful, Neal! You've shared so many actionable insights, but in closing, is anything else that you want to share? Any words of wisdom or inspiration?

No. I think working with you and your team, that people that become agents probably have a certain personality. They're probably more outgoing. I would assume that

that's part of the job is that they have to meet people. So, it's really taking who they are offline and putting it online. And I think if they can do that, they're already going to be ahead of the game and doing it not in an artificial way. We're going to be creating, training, and offering best practices, but it's really being who they are, being true to themselves. At the end of the day, people are going to do business, not with a photo on Instagram, but with you as a person. So, you need to be the same online that you are offline. You never want to be in the situation where, when someone knows you online and then meets you offline, they see that you completely different.

You don't want to become that person. So, it's not a lot of rocket science, it takes an initial part of education, and it takes consistency and really staying the course, but just being yourself and showing up online, it's not hard to do. You need to build a new habit just like when you started exercising an hour a day, you need to build that five, 10, 15 minutes a day to just monitor your social media what have you. But I think once you get into the habit, it becomes very natural. And I think it becomes over time, in this industry, it should become part of a very natural way of doing business in a post-pandemic economy. So, I'll leave it with that note.

STUART

Well, that's great, Neal. Thanks so much again for your time and your insights, and I know that our audience will really take a lot from it. So, thank you for that.

SCHAFFER

Oh, no worries. Thank you.

Chapter 8—
Influential Communication—
Words Matter

STUART

Allan, one reason I asked you to contribute to this section of the book on Real Estate Influence is that you are an Industry acknowledged expert on business-to-consumer communication. An additional reason is that when I introduce you at conventions and conferences, you always request that I introduce you as the Real Estate Industry's ONLY and, therefore, foremost DEMOTIVATIONAL speaker. I confess I had only heard of motivational speakers. Please explain what a demotivational or uninspiring speaker has to do with influence.

DALTON

Chris, I may be wrong, but I am convinced that a major reason why consumers lack greater respect for our industry is a direct consequence of how the real estate industry communicates and positions its overall value. Regrettably, much of the real estate industry's ritualistic rhetoric must be retooled. Clearly, many industry calcified cliches carry negative influence to the point where many consumers have figuratively speaking developed antibodies to much of this ill-advised and counterproductive communication that is crying out for a major dose of demotivation.

STUART

Very interesting perspective, Allan. Can you provide some specific examples of counterproductive communication Realtors® will employ?

Chris, before I provide a series of examples, I would like to share the research I have done regarding the most effective methods of negatively influencing or demotivating consumers. The four major methods of demotivation are through embarrassment, belittlement, self-focus, and prematurely attempting to change how consumers think.

STUART

Can you explain how certain words provide negative influence?

DALTON

Let me begin my assault on industry-wide communication by examining the use of one of the real estate industry's most cherished words, a word despised by many consumers, 'comps.' We should ask ourselves, "Why is it that, in an industry that recoils when all real estate agents are perceived by the public to all be the same, we actually employ the word 'comps' in an ill-fated attempt to convince homesellers that their home is similar to other homes?" My well-considered advice is that, unless the real estate industry is determined to win an unofficial confederation of dunces-like award, then the commoditized word 'comps' needs to be immediately purged.

STUART

Allan, what a sensational and demotivational indictment of that word. Explain the negative influence surrounding the word 'comps', and please offer a more positive and influential alternative.

DALTON

Chris, when a well-intentioned real estate agent myopically uses the word 'comps,' it is similar to saying, "Let's take a look at some similar children." Homesellers immediately confirm their displeasure by saying, "But that home doesn't have a swimming pool, and the other home does not have a new kitchen like we do." Attempting to force homesellers to prematurely accept what they do not think to be true, has a myriad of negative consequences, including their conclusion that any pricing recommendations to follow are invalid due to the agent's inability to grasp the distinctiveness of their home and lifestyle.

STUART

Allan, those are some compelling points, and I sense this is a perspective that has been largely overlooked. What is your alternative to the word 'comps?'

DALTON

A more influential way to make the same point would be: "Folks, let's review some of the properties that consumers will be evaluated at the same time they are assessing your home, but remember each home is distinctive. Based upon buyer behavior in today's market, where do you think we should price your home?" or, "Based upon buyer behavior in today's market, this is where I believe we should price your very distinctive home."

STUART

I love the difference, as instead of comparing homes, some of which the agent might have not even previewed, you are comparing buyer behavior and therefore removing the possibility of consumers feeling belittled or underappreciated. Allan, how about another industry cliché whose usage you would like to demotivate.

DALTON

The next wide-spread value killing cliché relates to the very essence of how real estate professionals function. The industry astonishingly still embraces the words 'listing presentation.' I ask, has there been a homeowner in history who has ever requested a listing presentation? Or would they prefer a 'marketing proposal?" I'll leave the verdict to the readers.

STUART

Allan, you know what some of the readers might think. This is just semantics, what say you?

DALTON

A homeseller can 'list' their home, and so can self-proclaimed discount companies. When agent value is reduced to a listing agent characterization and to one who makes listing presentations versus a marketing agent creating a collaboratively arrived at marketing proposal, then value and influence suffer.

STUART

Can you be more specific regarding the difference between a 'listing agent' and a 'marketing agent,' and a 'listing presentation' and a 'marketing proposal?' I want to ensure no one stills points to semantics.

The words 'listing agent' suggest one's job is complete once the listing has been secured. Chris, you and I know that the immensity of the tasks involved in marketing a home is far greater than merely securing the listing. A listing presentation is about the agent, their company, and their past success. To the contrary, a marketing proposal reflects the individual needs of the homeseller, their property, and what will be done in the future. A listing presentation is performative; a marketing proposal is collaborative. These nuances, as previously mentioned, are not merely a matter of semantics. These profound distinctions will determine whether consumers will either be positively or negatively influenced.

STUART

Powerful distinctions. What I am hearing you say is that doctors do not refer to fellow surgeons as medical people but instead opt to use their most elevated professional descriptions—surgeons. Therefore, why are skilled real estate professionals effectively stepping on their own air hoses by reducing their self-selected label as that of listing agents? Moreover, why are coaches and trainers still educating agents on how to make effective listing presentations? Allan, how about some additional examples of where real estate professionals need to be demotivated in order to increase their influence.

DALTON

Every trainer, broker, manager, coach, and agent I have known in this industry has said that, in real estate, "the market determines the price." I respectfully say they all need to be demotivated from that illogical and false belief. The market does not determine the price; it only influences the price. The price is instead determined by the following stakeholders - the buyer, the buyer agent, the seller, the seller agent, the lender, and the appraiser. Thank goodness for this reality, even though this realization has not yet reached the real estate industry. Real estate professionals should indeed be grateful that the market doesn't determine the price—because if real estate prices were determined by the market, as is the case with stocks or commodities, homesellers would naturally value a real estate transation in the same fasion as they view a daily stock trade. A friend of mine told me the other day that he sold one hundred thousand dollars worth of stock and was charged fifty dollars.

Have real estate professionals ever wondered why consumers believe agents have more to do with their home being sold than do stockbrokers in the sale of their stock? Here is the answer—because the market never determines the price of a home, it only influences the price. What else influences the price? The real estate agent, due to their influential staging, negotiating, networking, marketing, and selling skills, significantly determines and influences the price.

I suggest that each day of the year, every real estate agent in our prodigiously photoshopped profession, look in the proverbial mirror and shout "Hallelujah," celebrating that neither the market nor the buyer alone determines the price. Thankfully, homesellers appear to have a greater understanding of how real estate is not a commodity or stock, where the market completely determines the price, than the real estate industry. The real estate industry, in my opinion, ironically needs to arrive at least at the level of perceived value as that of homesellers versus its own self-limiting labels and definitions.

STUART

Allan, I love how you are identifying methods of increasing influence by first recognizing greater real estate agent value. I similarly speak to the relationship between agent value and influence in my chapter covering service, services, and skills. Where is the next area that we need, as you say, to "retool real estate rhetoric?"

DALTON

Chris, I have witnessed real estate speakers ask their agents to cry out the answer to why homes do not sell. The universal yet simplistically incorrect and influence killing answer is almost always 'price.' The influence-related problem here, is that if the only reason a home does not sell is due to price, then conversely, the only reason a home does sell must also be due to price. Should the only reason for a home not selling be attributable to price, then this leaves the greatest value of a real estate agent at the level of an appraiser, not to mention that three different appraisers typically arrive at three different pricing recommendations for the same property. And there is a reason why an appraiser is paid hundreds of dollars, and a marketing agent thousands or tens of thousands of individually negotiated dollars.

STUART

What is your reason for when homes do not sell?

DALTON

When homes do not sell, it is due to ineffective market-ing—because price is just a part of overall marketing. In the 1950s the Harvard Business School came out with the iconic 4Ps of marketing: price product placement and promotion. Most of the selling and marketing world embraced the clarity of this breakthrough explanation of marketing. The four P's revealed the interplay of each of these components and their distinct and interrelated roles in creating a sale. Unfortunately, the real estate industry seemingly ignored these basic business principles, perhaps viewing them as an inconvenient challenge to extend value.

STUART

Why do you think the real estate industry focused more on only one P— that being 'Price?'

DALTON

How better to ensure that every home in history that did not sell could never be attributed to the inadequate nego-tiating, staging, marketing, networking, or selling skills of the real estate agent? This behavior ensured that ho-mesellers, as they are involved in varying degrees of the pricing decision, would always be held more responsible than the 'listing agent.' The unintended consequences of where blame is placed is the all-time influence killer. This is because—if agents accept no blame for when homes do not sell, they should not expect to receive sufficient credit for when homes do sell.

STUART

In other words, if there were ineffective negotiating, staging, networking, or selling skills employed, it really did not matter. Thus, the only area of consequence, or where influence mattered, related to the home price being set low enough to ensure a sale.

DALTON

Exactly, Chris. Some of my former agents would say, "Allan, you could have five dead bodies in the basement, but if you lower the price enough, someone will still buy that home." Again, the pricing of the home effectively canceling out the need for any other professional influence or value. The agent's appraisal skill equals 100% influence; all other skills equal 0% influence when determining outcomes.

STUART

Allan, I love the advice you give agents when they are asked what makes them different than other agents.

DALTON

"Folks, rather than focusing on how I am different from other real estate agents, I want us to focus more on how we have to highlight what is different about your home. Please understand that I don't compete against other agents, as much as your home competes against other homes on the market. I actually cooperate with all of the other agents, as they and their companies will all be involved in my marketing plan, but the other homes on the market will in no way be cooperating with your home. Let me now show you how my marketing proposal will differentiate your home."

Allan, I've also heard you attack many of the typical responses agents deliver when they are asked, "How is the real estate market?"

Never say, "It's unbelievable!"—Just look up the meaning of that word.

Never say, "It's great!"—Great for who, the buyer or the seller?

Never say, "I've never been busier!"—That wasn't the question.

Never say, "All I need is a few more listings!"—That sounds like you are begging because no one else is using you.

Here is what I recommend instead, "Thanks for asking. We are in a very opportunistic market. There are great opportunities for buyers, sellers, and investors. Now let me ask you a question—When do you think you will be making your next real estate move?" Or for those real estate professionals who are most prepared and want to be trusted real estate advisors, a more 'advisor' response might be, "Thanks for asking. When I checked last night the listed homes here in town are down 15% from last year. Regarding days on market, the time before a sale is 35% less—at 47 days. We're continuing to see a significant degree of outward migration from the city. Buyers are willing to pay a premium for space, swimming pools, and home offices. Appreciation is up 8%. I'm concerned about future affordability—even though interest rates are historically low. So, for homeowners that intend on staying in their homes for 5 to 10 years, there isn't must statistical relevance here—but for anybody considering selling their home within the next year or two, my advice is "Sooner rather than later. By the way, if I recall correctly, you have a beautiful custom pool, don't you? Now I'd like to ask you a question. When do you think you'll be making your next real estate move?"

STUART

Allan, your response sounded more like a trusted advisor than "it's unbelievable." My next question is that real estate agents are constantly asked, as are all adults, 'What do they do for a living?' Do you have any demotivational words for us in that regard?

DALTON

Yes, let me demotivate the following—Never say, "I'm in real estate, but I used to be a teacher," or "I am in real estate, but I used to work for I.B.M.," or "I am in real estate, but I used to work for the government." These qualifying statements, which modify, and in some cases apologize for your career as a real estate professional, are akin to somebody saying, "I'd like you to meet my wife Alice, and also please say 'Hi' to my ex-wife Betty."

STUART

Allan, I know you have hundreds of examples of language that needs to be demotivated. How about some more.

Thousands of real estate professionals have copied this back of the business card prospecting ploy: The sincerest compliment somebody can pay me, is to send me referrals from their family and friends.

I recommend that be substituted with: My greatest professional privilege would be to serve the real estate needs of your family and friends.

STUART

How about another?

DALTON

A great way of demotivating people is to repeat what consumers say. As an example—some agents have been taught that when a potential buyer asks on the phone, "Does the home have four bedrooms?" to respond, "Do you want four bedrooms?" This would be similar to going into a restaurant that served pizza and asking if they have pepperoni pizza—then having to listen to this boomerang response, "Do you want pepperoni pizza?" Chris, I also recommend that real estate brokers consider shifting obsession with the words 'recruiting and retention' and replace them with 'selection and development.' The only other organizations who possess the same unyielding attachment to these words would be the military and their love of the word 'recruiting' and the penal system with its devotion to the word 'retention.' I also recommend that agents think in terms of building a 'client base' versus a 'data base' and stop thinking of SEO only in term of 'search engine optimization' and begin thinking of *seek engine optimization* — which means using advanced technologies such as Adwerx, Chalk-Digital, and Xpressdocs to insert influence with consumers before they search. And speaking of databases, I could have the largest database in California simply by purchasing the voter registration rolls from the Democratic and Republican parties and therefore walk through real estate conventions proud as a peacock, but if all I have is a database, within a year or two, I'll turn into a real estate feather duster.

I also firmly believe that the real estate industry, if it doesn't employ what I call 'seek engine optimization' to preempt 'search engine optimization' (SEO), that it will encounter cataclysmic consequences.

Chris, I hope that this small sample of more strategic words and phrases will be employed to replace some of the regrettable rhetoric promulgated within the real estate profession. The thoughts behind the words must be carefully examined. I've always appreciated the saying, "language is the clothing of ideas." In order for our words and communication to become more influential, it is required that our thoughts are influential.

Let me give you another example—Years ago, during my brokerage years, it once occurred to me that every other real estate company in North America was still using the letters C.M.A. representing a 'Comparative or Competitive Market Analysis.' Beyond the fact that properties compete, and not markets, I asked myself, "Should I just follow what everybody else does or might there be a more intelligent alternative?" Therefore, I created for my company the M.M.A. (Master Market Analysis) as opposed to a C.M.A.

Allan, what's the difference?

The C.M.A. is designed to conclude what the estimated fair market value of a property is. My M.M.A. or 'Master Market Analysis' was explained to homesellers as a method designed to not only help the client determine what their home was worth, but also added recommendations on how they could make their home worth more. This meant that I was able to have all of my associates point out to homesellers that if the homeseller went with any other company, and were actually only doing a C.M.A., that that was insufficient—because what was really needed was an M.M.A. So too, our industry seems to be in lock-step in its devotion to what is commonly referred to as 'Contact Management Systems.' Where I believe we should be communicating 'Content Management Systems.'

In fact, I believe that if there were a 'Do not be contacted by a real estate agent registry,' millions of homeowners would be standing in line to sign up. One has to wonder whether the consumer perceives one of the industry's favorite expressions, 'I Stay In Touch,' more as a threat than an announcement. Why? Because they want content more than contact—which is why they increasingly go to the internet before engaging their real estate agent.

Allan, do you have any science behind this?

Yes I do. During my several years as C.E.O. of Realtor. com, we used to track that very point. We had two tabs next to one another—one was titled 'Find a Home,' and the other was titled 'Find a Realtor.' 99% of the visitors to the site clicked on 'Find a Home' because they were looking for content. 1 % clicked on 'Find a Realtor,' and most of those who made that request were Realtors® checking on their profile information—which gave me the science, Chris, to emphatically proclaim that, ***"Where the real estate industry needs to go to have more influence regarding information is communication through consumer-centric content which will lead to relational contacts."***

Chapter 9—
Becoming More Influential
with and For Homesellers

The preponderance of content within *Real Estate Influence* concerns itself with how real estate agents can optimize their professional influence. This chapter extends the importance of maximizing influence to include the pursuit of listings and the effective marketing of properties on behalf of homesellers.

I have invited Allan Dalton to advance his suggestions and strategies regarding how to both present to and represent homesellers more effectively and influentially than the real estate industry's conventional approaches.

I have seen documentation from the following national brands that cite Allan as being either the developer or co-developer of their organization's marketing systems. These national companies include Better Homes and Gardens, Century 21, Coldwell Banker, ERA, Berkshire Hathaway HomeServices, and Real Living.

STUART

Allan, there must be a common theme that connects all of your systems.

DALTON

Chris, there are fundamental beliefs that both define and differentiates each marketing presentation and system. One essential tenet is that real estate professionals should forego and forget the words "listing presentation." A list-

ing presentation immediately connotes self-focus, inse-
curity, and inadequately reflects the greater and often
overlooked value of a real estate marketing professional.
Purging these industry-wide fancied and favored words
requires shifting one's professional "why."

My strongly recommended conversion must constitute a
departure from self-identified listing agents subjecting homesellers to performative listing presentations—directed
towards extolling their virtues and accomplishments and
what makes them different from other agents—to instead
displaying a laser-like focus on that which makes the
home different from competitive homes and how to leverage and showcase that distinctiveness through customized
marketing.

STUART

Allan, that sounds like common sense. Yet, as Frank
Lloyd Wright famously said, "There is nothing more uncommon than common sense." Allan, when did you first
realize the difference between a listing presentation and
a marketing proposal, and how the emphasis should be
placed on what makes a property different — even more so
than what makes the agent and their company different?

DALTON

Chris, necessity was my mother of invention. When I
moved from Boston to New Jersey to join Murphy Realty
Better Homes and Gardens, I was hired and compensated
for two reasons. The first was to increase the listing inventory of the company. The second was to, along with
Joe Murphy, the founder and chairman of the company,

to grow our brokerage. When I arrived with my family in New Jersey, our company had only three offices in the state. Our two chief competitors, Weichert and Schlott — each had approximately one hundred offices in the Garden State alone—and were both at the several billion dollars plus level in transactional volume.

STUART

I know that those two companies, along with Long and Foster, were the three largest independent brokerages at that time in America, if not the world. Therefore, how did you compete in your marketing presentations against their listing presentations, beyond the cliché, "We give better (or more personal) service"?

DALTON

We competed during marketing presentations success-fully due to the so-called mother of invention. For twen-ty years, I made ten or more marketing presentations per week. I did so while accompanying colleagues among our twelve hundred plus sales executives. Although Joe and I owned thirty-two offices and managed twenty-eight affiliates, at the time we sold the company, we were never anywhere close statistically to Weichert or Schlott.

Also, our brand Better Homes and Gardens wasn't as large as many of the other brands in our market. Consequently, how could I possibly make a competitive and compelling listing presentation? What homeseller would be im-pressed by a listing presentation featuring a company with 80% less sales, and upon meeting an agent who needed me to accompany him or her, or with my Boston accent, since I was now in New Jersey?

To successfully secure listings, for our agents and my company, I had to first make our company "more listable." I did this by creating a marketing system, marketing proposals, and creating a full-page ad thirty years ago that introduced to the public the Murphy Marketing System. My provocative ads included numerous other company's signs as part of our system.

Our for sale sign appeared in the middle of the ad, with all the competitors' signs respectfully showcased as supportive satellites, comprising important components of the Murphy Home Marketing System. Homesellers rewarded our agents and company for the full transparency in these ads revealing how real estate was truly marketed.

By virtue of my company monumentally celebrating cooperation and that real estate agents operate more as symphony conductors orchestrating a collaborative system versus virtuosos. It worked remarkably well for us—given our significantly smaller market share.

It immediately provided our three offices, when our system was first introduced, plausibility when going against one hundred densely located competitor offices.

STUART

When you showed me those ads that displayed all of your competitors for sale signs in the newspaper, I wondered, did any of them complain?

143

The companies that I included were too stunned to complain. They instead experienced a sort-of approach-avoidance conflict. On the one hand, I believe they felt a subliminal thrill over receiving free advertisements of their company's yard signs. Conversely, perhaps they were somewhat traumatized through their full-frontal realization that I had just strategically co-opted them and their influence. Ironically, the only complaints I did receive were from some of the smaller companies. Understandably, these were less known brokerages who were outraged that they did not make the A-list.

STUART

What did your agent say to homesellers during marketing presentations when homesellers mentioned competitive companies?

DALTON

Over the years, which is equally pertinent today and will be ten years from now, all our agents learned to say, "these other companies were already part of our marketing system, and since no company sells more than 10% of the homes in the state, no company, therefore, was large enough, which means that there must be a home marketing system that marshals cooperation and collaboration." Every real estate agent essentially knows this to be true but oftentimes their self-focused listing presentations under-stress this monumental fact. I have always believed that "Nothing matters until you make it matter" and without question, the best way to eliminate all competition is to manifest the highest level of passion in including them.

For example, any time a homeseller said, "I think your company is too small." The response I socialized throughout our whole company was, "Every real estate company is too small," followed by, "Let me show you how our marketing system operates, essentially, as one large company— in fact, the largest company serving you!"

STUART

What an ingenious way to leverage the influence of all your competitors by reminding homesellers that all of these other companies would become part of your influencer system on their behalf. Yet, what would you say if the homeseller said, "Well if these other companies are part of your marketing system, then you must be part of their marketing system."

DALTON

Chris, I would say, "Exactly. It's great that you understand how real estate marketing works." By having this conversation, it effectively neutered all competition, leaving the decision regarding representation to the merits of my one agent and our company's marketing system.

STUART

Let's now move on to the marketing proposal itself. Before you discuss how real estate professionals should deliver influential marketing, what is the best way for them to become immediately influential with the homesellers?

Becoming influential with and for homesellers begins with a real estate agent first determining their "why." Disturbingly, what I heard from some of my agents while driving to marketing presentation appointments over the years, reflected the wrong "why." These were colleagues who made negative comments about the homeseller or their properties before we arrived.

For example, "Allan, the husband is a real beaut," or, "This home has this problem or that problem," or, "These folks are delusional about what their home is worth."

Now even if these characterizations were all true, I detected at times, disdain and even disgust directed towards these unsuspecting homesellers. Perhaps these unflattering assessments were caused as these characterizations— that being a perceived lack of an appreciative homeseller— served as an anticipated threat to a potential commission.

"In other words, if the homesellers don't become more realistic with the price, their home will never sell, I will never receive a commission, and therefore I resent them for doing this to me."

It would be similar to a doctor mocking a patient they had just met in the hospital to another physician, "Wait until you meet my patient in room 4C; he thinks he is a lot healthier than he is."

STUART

What do these pre-appointment thoughts and comments, unbeknownst to you say to the homeseller, and what do they have to do with being influential with homeseller clients?

DALTON

According to research, the first question prospective clients ponder is," Do I like the salesperson?" Therefore, how can an agent positively influence a homeseller if they are carrying negative vibes into a meeting? They are left with only one alternative—fake respect for the homesellers and pretend enthusiasm for their home.

STUART

Allan, while you were listening to these disrespectful preludes to marketing presentations, what were you thinking?

DALTON

I was reminding myself of how I was going to love these people. They are providing my agent and company with an opportunity to serve them. They are also enabling us to shine, display marketing, networking, negotiating, staging skills, and earn a living. I intuitively understood that the only way I could have the homesellers like me—and therefore my company—was for me to first like them. Clearly, if I were feeling or bringing any negativity towards them or their property, it would be revealed, and my influence would be undermined. The homesellers would sense negative sentiments, and in a perverse example of the principle of reciprocity, return them in kind.

Interestingly, after securing the agreement to market the homeseller's property, while driving back to one of our offices with my now wildly enthusiastic and grateful colleague, and after being invited by these homesellers I had never met before to attend their upcoming wedding, bar mitzvah or party, my agents oftentimes would say the following, "Allan, I think these homesellers fooled you. They are really not that nice."

The reason I created influence is that the homesellers sensed that the way I felt about them would also lead to similar invitations from me to them. Plus, I did not use words like "comps" or that "the buyer determines the price" which would basically be like saying, "your home is like all others, and therefore, neither you nor I will have any negotiating impact."

Chris, you've heard me say this many times. Using the word "comps" with homesellers immediately destroys all influence because it's the same as saying, "Let's take a look at some comparable children." Leading the homeseller to conclude, "If the real estate agent doesn't even understand what makes our home different from all others, how can we ever be influenced by their pricing recommendation."

STUART

Allan, I completely agree that the first question that prospects in any sales or consultative setting ask themselves is, "Do I like the salesperson?" I also agree with the saying, "That we only have one chance to make a first impression." For a real estate professional to be influential with a homeseller, it clearly means making a positive initial impression. Therefore, during your hundreds upon hundreds of marketing presentations, how did you manage the first impression you made each time?

DALTON

The first impression for many homesellers, of my colleagues and I, was how we would never ring the doorbell without first taking sufficient time perusing the outside of the home. I would use a yellow pad of paper and make notes of what might be the first impression of the home among buyers and buyer agents. I would do this whether or not homesellers were aware of this practice. Homesellers oftentimes told me they appreciated that. Even before meeting me, I was already taking note of how to best showcase their property. Routinely taking the time to first contemplate the home's curb appeal and how it could be improved put me into the mode of already representing the property before I even met with the homesellers.

STUART

Allan, how do you communicate to homesellers the need for changes, improvements, or staging?

DALTON

Great question, Chris. Any suggested changes must be announced with meticulous sensitivity, surgeon-like skill and should be contextual in order to be influential.

STUART

Can you give me an example of what you mean by contextual?

The "contextualization of critiques" begins by first asking the homeseller to take a joint tour of their property
to determine and discuss which of their home's amenities will provide their home with the greatest marketing
advantage. What typically happens during the tour is
that homesellers inevitably point out improvements or
renovations. This is the time when homesellers should be
deservedly praised. Homesellers should be honored for
intelligently merchandising and increasing their home's
value. For example, should a homeseller say, "Allan, we
changed the cement surrounding the swimming pool to
blue slate and the sliding glass doors to French doors," I
always believed they deserved to hear more than just, "Oh,
that looks beautiful."

Instead, I would accurately and appropriately say, "Your
renovation is going to provide me with a marketing advantage over competitive homes. By the way, whose idea was
it to make this change?"

STUART

Allan, I think I know where you are going. By praising,
where warranted, remarkable features, you are commend-
ing the homesellers for their decision. Such recognition of
the steps taken by the homeseller to enhance their home's
value now makes it more contextually acceptable when
you have to suggest sensitive pricing information or other
changes to the home. This is because you are beginning by
celebrating "good news." Also, when you ask whose idea

was the improvement, and one of the sellers claims attribution, in a sense, it is almost like you are honoring and redeeming the value of their decision. But now, let's hear how you bring up negatives.

DALTON

The key is for the agent to not be the source of the negative—effectively guaranteeing they become the "bearer of bad news." Instead, after praising the praiseworthy, it is now more acceptable to encourage homesellers to admit the negatives or have the negatives come in the form of potential buyer agent criticism.

STUART

Allan, let's hear how this might take place.

DALTON

Chris, at the beginning of any marketing presentation, every marketing agent should ask homesellers either:
• what they like most about their home
• what they will miss most about their home/lifestyle, or
• what they think the new buyers will enjoy most when living in their home

When the homeseller has observed their marketing agent approvingly taking notes in front of the home, complimenting them on improvements, and now giving them the opportunity to effusively characterize the distinctiveness of their home, they are more open and less defensive in receiving staging related suggestions. My mother used to tell me that you can say anything as long as you employ the right timing and tone.

Here is my recommendation regarding improvement suggestions:

"Folks, now that we have reviewed all the many reasons why buyers would be fortunate to live here, and identified your distinct lifestyle amenities which will provide us with significant marketing advantages and a competitive edge, is there anything about your property that you can think of, that a buyer or a buyer agent might seize upon to bring down your home's value. If there is, let's strategize on how we will respond."

STUART

Allan, it sounds like you and the clients are becoming as one. You clearly are teaming up with the homesellers, preparing to validate value when challenged by the buyer and buyer agent. What if the homeowner doesn't volunteer any critical points?

DALTON

Your communication should be both sensitive and respectful:

"Folks, I don't believe in the word 'comps.' I believe that every lifestyle is distinctive. Homes do not compare—they compete. I want to go online and show you homes that buyers in your price range will be evaluating while also assessing the value of your property. Let's determine if there are any features of these homes that we can learn from regarding how they compete with yours. For example, a lot of the agents that have been to this home that we see can see online have complained that there was too much clutter, too many personal photos, or an overabundance of religious artifacts and political affiliation notices. This hyper-personalization is wonderful when living in a home, but not so when selling a home. Let's review your home and see if there are any changes that we can reasonably make that will increase its salability while at the same time maintaining your home's wonderful distinctiveness and character. Here are some of the changes that I believe will broaden the appeal and increase the demand for your home."

STUART

Allan, you have covered the "why," what to do outside the home, and what to say when you first meet the homesellers while touring the home; please share how you recommend a marketing agent begin their marketing presentation or proposal.

DALTON

During all my years making marketing presentations or proposals, after touring the home, rejoicing and validating their improvements, and then moving to a place for the presentation, before sitting down, I would always ask the homesellers, "Can I take another look at the backyard or patio?" My purpose was that by leaving the room, it provided homesellers the opportunity to share their initial feelings about me.

Oftentimes homesellers, before our appointment, agree with one another that they should not sign anything that night. I refer to this as their consumer covenant or seller's pact.

STUART

I like that idea, Allan, because it gives homesellers some time, in the same way that doctors and other professionals also offer their patients private time to temporarily be alone. This provides the opportunity for them to hopefully agree that they like the agent because of all of the behavioral steps that you outlined. What a great way for them to overtly give each other permission that should they continue to be this impressed, they can now sign that evening. Allan, what is the next step?

DALTON

"Folks, tonight I have brought some pricing and marketing strategies. Which would you like to cover first?"

STUART

What I like about the way you are beginning, Allan, is that this approach eliminates the possibility of homesellers interrupting the beginning of a presentation. For example, "Can we just get to the price?" or "You don't have to sell us on yourself." Also, this communication is very consultative. This is because you are asking a question which displays confidence. Your method also displays that you are completely secure and comfortable surrounding both subjects and ready to discuss them in the preferred order of the homesellers, "What if the homeseller says can we start with the price?"

DALTON

Chris, I believe that in order to optimize one's influence, and thus professional value with homesellers, the discussion of price must begin by acknowledging the importance

of seven questions which govern how a real estate professional should introduce the subject of price:

1. What percentage of real estate agents overprice their
personal residence?

2. What percentage of real estate agents have access to all
the relevant real estate pricing data?

3. Therefore, why don't real estate agents rely upon this
data when pricing their personal residence?

4. What percentage of homesellers are enthusiastic about
the data?

5. When homesellers are not immersed in joy over the
data, does this cause the agent to be viewed as the bearer
of bad news?

6. Is there any truth to the adage, "shoot the messenger?

7. What percentage of homesellers have a price in mind
before the agent even arrives?

STUART

Allan, I think I know, but I would like to hear it from you.
What do these pricing strategy-related questions tell us?

DALTON

It reminds us that if real estate professionals, who possess all the data still cannot escape their own subjectivity,
delusions, and even greed, why then would the real estate
industry ever myopically believe that consumers will?

Therefore, why should any real estate professional begin a conversation regarding pricing strategies based upon data? Chris, as we both agree, knowledge and wisdom present greater value than information and data. While data is still indispensable, a knowledgeable professional, before introducing data, must first tenderize homesellers by reminding the homesellers that their job is not that of an appraiser declaring the price. Rather their role as a trusted advisor is to collaborate with their clients on the determination of the appropriate "pricing strategy." Such strategy must not only be based upon data but the knowledge, wisdom, marketing, and negotiating skill of the agent, along with the circumstances and the threshold of the homesellers regarding the uncertainty of the outcome.

STUART

Allan, I like your distinction between an appraiser and a real estate agent, especially when considering that if you have multiple appraisers, you generally have multiple estimates of fair market value. There is a major reason why homesellers pay real estate professionals much more than appraisers, which must be reflected throughout the pricing process. What do you suggest as an alternative opening to the subject of price?

DALTON

Rather than appearing as an advocate for one's research and thereby polarizing the agent and the homeseller, the subject of pricing should be first introduced in more of a collaborative and consultative fashion. To avoid becoming the bearer of bad news, here is my suggested method:

"Folks, I provide my clients with three distinct pricing strategies from which to choose. Strategy number 1 is for clients who choose to select the data approach to pricing. These are clients who elect to have their home priced based upon what the data will support. When I mention data, I am referring to what we call a CMA or an appraisal. The reason why some homesellers select this strategy is to ensure, to the degree possible, that their property will appraise out. They also don't want to offend the pricing sensibilities of buyers and buyer agents.

Pricing strategy number 2 is the 'less is more' pricing strategy. This is where homesellers desire to price their property lower than the data would support. Their motive is to significantly increase demand and competition.

The third pricing strategy I refer to as the 'retail pricing strategy.' This pricing strategy is to accommodate clients who desire to price their property reasonably higher than the data would support. Their pricing strategy anticipates that buyers, especially in certain markets, will automatically offer less money than the asking price. Therefore, this strategy builds in a negotiating cushion.

Of these three pricing strategies, which seems philosophically to make the most sense to you, folks?"

STUART

I love that consultative, collaborative, and knowledge-based approach. It reflects an inclusive "pricing strategy" rather than unilateral dictating a subjectively determined price. However, I don't think there's a magic wand that leads to any and all properties being appropriately priced. Where does your consultative approach go next?

DALTON

Homesellers that I approached with this method over the years typically responded in one of two ways. Either with, "Well, what are we talking about? What does the data show?" or "Well, that's why we are hiring you! what do you think?" These two inevitable responses are precisely the rationale that form this pricing method. Intentionally, I have involved the homesellers as part of the strategic pricing process. I offered them a choice in the same way a physician might offer different therapies. This consultative approach earns their trust. On display is how I am there to represent them. It becomes clear that I am not there merely to robotically regurgitate accumulated data used to inspire subjective and one-sided conclusions.

Once it has been established that I am not there solely as a disciple of software spreadsheets that never take into account home interiors or landscaping nuances, I can now move on in a fashion that is different than most real estate agents. That would be real estate professionals who have been coached to begin the pricing process by astonishingly presenting their CMA. After first engaging homesellers on mutually discussed strategies, I then introduce data. I believe this more sophisticated and consumer-respectful method, where consumers become a vital part of the decision-making process, as opposed to listening to dogmatic and subjective conclusions, dramatically builds trust and mutual comfort. This advanced method also reduces the likelihood that homesellers will seek different pricing opinions. This is because they will have been converted into participants of this opinion process.

A process, while still fully relying upon data, does so contextually, consultatively, and conversationally rather than the homeowners painfully listening to a software-driven commentary.

STUART

Allan, I am confident that the real estate agents who read this book will love your methodology. I agree that this sophisticated approach to the sensitive subject of pricing will cause any and all homesellers to view them as more influential and trustworthy.

Since you have covered the pricing, what if the homesellers choose to begin with marketing, or when you introduce marketing after you have covered pricing?

DALTON

Chris, let me assume that I have already covered price.

"Folks, I believe if we bring your property to the market at the price we have agreed upon, it will reflect a very optimistic price. As I have said, we don't want to put your property on the market at the highest possible price, but rather the highest realistic price. I believe that the price we have selected does represent the highest realistic price. I will do everything in my power to validate and support this price. If we are not successful in commanding this price, however, we will then have to adjust the price. Should we have to adjust the price in the future, I am confident that it would not be because of my marketing. After we now review my marketing strategy for your home, you will understand why I say this."

STUART

Allan, I like what I am hearing. You did not say, "We can try it at that price," which is like somebody saying, "We can give marriage a try." I also like how you pointed out that you are all in. I also took note that you explained to the homesellers that if the home doesn't sell at that price, it won't be because of the marketing. What a dramatic and confident way to set the foundation for your marketing conversation or presentation, as well as impressing the homeseller with the vital importance of marketing. I'm ready to hear how you will introduce marketing.

DALTON

"Folks, (or Susan and John, or whoever), all real estate marketing comes down to three words: range, reach, and influence.

Range represents the internet. Essentially all real estate companies and consumers enjoy internet access.

Reach refers to the extent of the exposure. Not every person or product that goes on the internet enjoys the same reach, even though there is only one internet. The real estate industry enjoys immense reach because of how we exchange our homes for sale information with essentially all other real estate firms. This means that all the other companies in our marketplace that belong to the MLS will have the pictures and the words that you and I select together featured on their website as well. Is that exciting or what?

Influence is most vital because we want to ensure that after buyers are exposed to your property, on either the internet, through social media, local marketing, open houses, etc., that they will be influenced to not only want to buy your home but also at the highest realistic price. This means we must also influence buyer agents. Therefore, our marketing strategy and my marketing plan must ensure a high level of influence on behalf of your home. Influence surrounding your lifestyle and home for sale, off and online, begins with you influencing me. As part of my marketing plan, I first need to know the many reasons why you folks believe buyers would want to live here.

STUART

Allan, I'm very impressed with how you eliminate the competition by including them, as the proper introduction of IDX will do. I'm not going to ask you to go any deeper into the rest of the dialogue you have created for our networks, but I will ask you, "How do you close the marketing proposal?"

DALTON

"John and Susan, based upon the price that we have discussed, and all of the components of my marketing system, in your opinion, do you believe that I can do an effective job of marketing your home?"

At this time, the homesellers universally, from my experience and in my opinion, will always say "yes." How can they say anything but, especially as I have deservedly honored them, their home, their improvements, involved them in the pricing strategy, eliminated the competition by including them, discussed how we will overcome buyer objections, and revealed everything I will do off and online to increase their range, reach, and influence? Therefore, here is the close that follows my trial close, "All I have is one last question—how soon would you like to have your remarkable home sold to the right buyer?"

Whether their answer is "in a week," "a month," or "by the end of spring, summer, fall or winter," my last response is always the same—"Great, then let's get started. It's an honor to represent you," and with a big pre-covid handshake, "Thank you for selecting me."

STUART

Allan, thank you so much for sharing what you have learned over so many years. What I love about what you have reviewed—and that's without even getting into your amazing creative marketing solutions that I don't want you to share outside of our networks—that dedication towards expanding one's influence should never be separated from the need to influence buyer and buyer-agents through maximizing reach, range, and influence in order to deliver great outcomes for one's clients and your communities. I love where you've taken our conversation, as this chapter isn't intended to be about influence marketing; it's about influencing homesellers. The questions for our readers are:

• How can we expect to influence homesellers if we use a word like 'comps' and try to force homesellers to conceived that their home is similar to others?

• How can we expect to influence homesellers if our pricing spreadsheets were not properly introduced?

• How can we influence home sellers if we convert them into 'listing presentation victims' as opposed to 'marketing presentation collaborators'?

• How can we influence homesellers if we focus more on how we're different than celebrating that which makes their home different?

• How can we influence homesellers if we don't honor their home and their improvements or, privately mock their natural human desire to receive more money from the sale?

Great concepts about influencing homesellers, Allan!

DALTON

Happy to share them, Chris!

Chapter 10—
Influential Selling

Who is the greatest salesperson you have ever worked with, for, or observed? The answer for me is my former boss, Larry Ellison, the legendary CEO and co-founder of Oracle. For anyone who struggles characterizing this giant influencer of the evolution of technology as a 'salesperson,' I invite you to Google the Business Insider article written by Eugene Kim. This article features billionaires who significantly owe their success to their sales ability. One of my many reasons for turning to Salesforce for their CRM solutions is due to the selling ability of their founder and CEO, Marc Benioff. Although Marc majored in business administration in college, and Larry in science, these two exalted examples from what Eugene Kim refers to as 'The Billionaires Club,' along with fellow past member Steve Jobs, owe much of their stratospheric success to not just their technology and management brilliance but also their ability to persuade, sell, and influence.

Marc Benioff attributes much of his ability to sell concepts and solutions to his mentor Larry Ellison. Larry Ellison was a mentor of mine as well. I immediately took note, upon arriving at Oracle, that Mr. Ellison, although we clearly had nothing in common in terms of wealth, and I both had a science background and shared a similarity in one aspect of our family backgrounds. Not lost on me was that I never met my biological father, and Larry Ellison never met his biological mother until he reached the age of 28. The reason I begin this chapter examining the relationship between selling and real estate influence by citing examples of cultural and economic game changers is that they are also considered 'world-class salespeople.' How their selling ability enables them to sell solutions to the world causes me to question how real estate professionals view themselves. As you answer the question, "Who is the greatest salesperson you know," I also ask you to consider whether you admire or disrespect that individual. I believe the manner in which you perceive other salespeople influences your self-perception as a salesperson. Such internalization or salesperson-related self-image may very well influence your ability to sell or persuade others.

The next greatest salesperson I have known is Gino Blefari. Gino is the CEO of HomeServices of America and Chairman of HSF Affiliates. Gino, long before achieving his lofty executive status, became the number 1 real estate salesperson in Santa Clara County, California. Gino went on to "sell" thousands of agents on working with him as he lead the largest and most successful Century 21 company, at that time, in the world. His selling, persuasion, and influencing skills, along with his well-established leadership, were once more called upon as he built Intero Real Estate along with his partners. Intero, according to Real Trends rankings, during Gino's tenure, became one of the real estate industry's top 10 brokerages. Those who know Gino well, as I do, may first characterize Gino in one of the following ways—a great leader, a consummate executive, a brilliant strategist, an indefatigable networker, a respected teacher, or humanitarian. All of these descriptions, in my view, are apt and accurate. I also believe that Gino would be the first to acknowledge that at the very foundation of the vast value he has brought to the real estate industry would be his career-long dedication to the art of selling, persuasion, and influence.

Gino can point to the hundreds of books on selling, including *How to Win Friends and Influence People*, as bedrocks that have influenced his strategic personal development and considerable success. In fact, the statement "considerable success" is an understatement as many people refer to Gino Blefari as the real estate industry's GOAT (greatest of all time). I am writing this chapter during a time where the NFL's Tom Brady has only strengthened his being defined as football's GOAT by virtue of his team's winning seven Super Bowls with him being named The Super Bowl MVP five times. Sports writers are acknowledging that if you divided this legendary quarterback's career into three distinct time periods, he would be a first ballot Hall of Famer each of the three times. Gino Blefari is the only individual I know who also would be worthy of selection as a three time first ballot Hall of Famer in real estate. When one considers Gino's many years as the number one producing agent in Santa Clara County, the number one president of all Century 21 companies worldwide, and his first ballot Hall of Fame-worthy years as a CEO—first at Berkshire Hathaway HomeServices and now HomeServices of America—it certainly makes Gino not your ordinary Hall of Famer. Even more remarkable is that while Tom Brady achieved all of his success in one position, as quarterback, Gino's parthenon-like accomplishments would be the equivalent of someone succeeding at the highest level at three positions. First as a player, then as a coach, and finally as an owner. None of these achievements would have been possible if Gino didn't develop himself into a world-class salesperson. The reason I am weaving a thread between great leaders from different companies and sectors, and their ability to sell, is purposeful. Just as Larry Ellison, Steve Jobs, Marc Benioff, and Gino Blefari represent much more than salespeople, they are/were each very much a salesperson.

"How much of You—is a Salesperson?"

Specifically, where do your sales skills rank in your hierarchy of value? Are you more a negotiator, a networker, a marketeer, a prospector, a social media savant, or a world-class salesperson? Unlike CPAs, engineers, dentists, teachers, police officers, doctors, or nurses—in order to optimize your real estate influence—the development and interplay of all of these skills are indispensable. Interestingly, the significance, value, and perceived influence surrounding the value of real estate-related selling skills have waned in recent years. For example, I am told that 30 and 40 years ago, at real estate conventions, almost every exhibit booth was devoted to either 'how to list' or 'sell.' Back then, and before today's aisle upon aisle showcasing of software solutions, mobile technology, CRM programs, varieties of video programs, postcards, mortgage information, title companies, and coaching programs, a real estate agent could not walk more than five feet without an invitation to purchase tapes on selling. A gallery of 'selling gurus' included Tommy Hopkins, Danielle Kennedy, Mike Ferry, Floyd Wickman, Brian Tracy, Zig Ziglar, and Og Mandino, the self-proclaimed 'world's greatest salesperson,' were the real estate rock stars of that era. In recent times, it appears that the importance of, and devotion to, 'selling' has become more the domain of billionaire tech icons and their minions at convention booths selling the real estate industry on their solutions. Less emphasis is evident when it comes to teaching real estate professionals to better sell their value and increase their influence.

One can only wonder if the real estate industry is 'devolving' from selling others to being sold.

The days in which the real estate industry was universally focused on how to close the sale, trial close, verify and reverse objections, execute tie-downs, the "feel, felt, found" technique, selling chains of conviction, perfect take away selling, consultative selling, feature advantage and benefit selling seem distant memories. Dale Carnegie's Sales Effectiveness courses, and Brian Tracy's Psychology of Selling, have also given way to being sold on social networking, artificial intelligence, CRM's, databases, being coached on business planning, and mobile app marketing. All of these modern-day activities are not only vital but imperative for real estate success. So too, selling skills due to their relationship to influence should be rekindled and reinvigorated. With only 7% of Americans each year transacting real estate, there is clearly room to rachet up persuasiveness, selling, and overall influence. Elevating selling, however, for many, may first require rigorous introspection. The question is, "What are the true feelings of real estate professionals about selling in general?"

I once heard that over 80% of real estate salespeople come into the industry without prior career selling experience.

This would be like hiring a team of engineers without any of the candidates ever being exposed to math.

Another factor impeding the industry's devotion to professional selling has been the introduction of automated technology and less direct personal engagement. Additionally, the bias much of society has against the word "salesperson" is also a factor in the real estate industry's relationship to the word selling. Ask yourself, have you ever said or thought, "I don't like it when somebody tries to sell me something." How do you believe that reaction to a salesperson trying to sell you something influences your willingness to sell something to someone else? Moreover, when you were in elementary school, and asked by your teacher, "What do you want to do when you grow up?" if you were like me, you probably responded with one of the following job or career selections: a teacher, an astronaut, an engineer, a professional athlete, etc. Can you recall many of your future-looking classmates announcing their intentions to someday be a salesperson? There would be far less bias towards selling if high school and college students were informed that professional selling is responsible for more millionaires than most other professions. If this were the case, then perhaps more individuals would plan on a sales career, versus too often seeking a career that is defined more as one of marketing and technology.

Many salespeople fail to appreciate that selling is a science, as is influence. Why is it that we still hear the expression that he or she is a natural-born salesperson? Less likely to be heard is the expression that somebody is a natural-born doctor, lawyer, engineer, CPA, or dentist. Little wonder why there is so little attention to professional selling skill development when the possession of such skills is positioned as something you are either born with or don't have. This distinction between 'born a salesperson' or 'developing world-class selling skills' is also evident in how many individuals do not grasp the profound difference between hard-selling, consultative selling, and no selling.

Hard selling is similar to what I discuss in my chapter on influential marketing. I point out the difference between inside-out and outside-in marketing. Inside-out is when a salesperson or company determines what they would like to sell and how it addresses their needs, whereas outside-in marketing first determines the needs of the consumer and then presents solutions that lead to mutual understanding and respect.

Inside-out selling is when a salesperson tries to do the impossible. Manipulate, control, or force a consumer or client to make a decision which they do not perceive is in their best interest. We have all heard of the WIFM principle. Although I always endeavor to avoid cliches, this 'what's in it for me' axiom causes hard selling to almost always fail.

Consultative selling, or value-based selling, is where the salesperson engages the prospect, customer, or client based upon their needs versus the need to sell a product or service. Since the science of selling indicates that consumers buy emotionally, but justify logically, means that consumers are not able to logically justify their decisions based upon hard-sell or inside-out selling. Only through asking relevant questions, listening, displaying empathy, and through reflection or restatement can the professional salesperson reach the level of effective persuasiveness, selling, and ultimately influence that is required to consummate a sale.

Also included in the three alternatives is 'no selling.'

This category describes so-called real estate salespeople, who, when asked, "How's the real estate market?", as Allan Dalton mentions in my interview with him on communication, actually answer, "It's unbelievable." That non-answer represents 'no selling.' Not hard selling, not consultative selling, but 'no selling.' Another example is when a homebuyer tells the buyer agent that they are not interested in a home, and the buyer agent immediately begins lining up other homes to show, versus professionally meeting, verifying, and reversing concerns in order to help their buyer client approach a buying decision from a more nuanced and profound place. A non-salesperson goes through their career believing that homes sell themselves. Therefore, stripping themselves of all influence. Even worse, a hard-selling salesperson attempts to override objections versus contextualizing concerns, which also destroys their potential influence.

The consultative salesperson compassionately and skillfully listens and then helps their buyer or seller arrive at the best conclusion.

Consultative salespeople, those who enjoy the greatest level of influence, appreciate that their approach to the sales process is not based upon a so-called sixth sense or intuition. They instead recognize that success means being guided by their knowledge, wisdom, empathy, and highly honed selling skills.

Clearly, an untrained salesperson, when told by a buyer they don't like the landscaping or kitchen, intuitively envisions alternative homes to show. Conversely, the professionally trained salesperson first verifies the concern or objection by saying, "If you weren't concerned about the landscaping or the kitchen, let's say they were more to your liking, then in your opinion, do you feel this home might meet your needs?" To which the buyer may respond, "We still wouldn't want to buy this home because we want to wait until next year anyway." This skillfully induced revelation saves the salesperson days, if not weeks, of driving through several communities in search of the ever-elusive perfect home that never would have mattered anyway. The non-salesperson does not verify the objection, the hard-selling salesperson tries to overcome the objection, and the professionally trained salesperson verifies the objection, thereby sensitively inserting realism and therefore trusted influence into the interaction.

The purpose of this chapter is not that it serves as a tutorial on selling—although not showcased at most convention booths, there is a voluminous library of non-industry-related books on selling that you can find online. In order to maximize real estate influence, for many real estate professionals, it will mean not only devoting greater attention to effectively engaging more consumers through social media, personal promotion, mobile marketing, and prospecting, but even more significantly, how you effectively serve, sell, and influence all those you engaged.

I respectfully suggest that not enough real estate professionals perceive the selling of real estate as a personal mission to help consumers.
I say this because if within the DNA of all real estate professionals was the determination to influence consumers instead of waiting to merely assist consumers after they have been influenced elsewhere, then we would have more agents doing more to promote the need to go from renting to buying, to move-up, to right size or downsize, to renovate, to sell, buy, or invest in real estate in general. These activities would trump the alternative—forever waiting to be approached or relying upon paying for leads. Real Estate professionals need to be forever selling and not forever waiting.

There are countless real estate agents who would willingly and even enthusiastically knock on the door of a stranger to influence or sell them on donating to a charity or keeping a cell phone tower out of a neighborhood. That same proactive real estate professional, too often, is not as willing to knock on a door or call a for-sale-by-owner or expired listing homeseller because a 'missionary zeal' is not to be found. The reason for this lack of feeling 'one is on a mission' is because the behavior is viewed differently than one is 'selling' a charity. Selling a charity to many is not perceived as a display of self-interest, whereas to some, encouraging consumers to consider or reconsider real estate activity is perceived as self-serving and therefore shunned by countless real estate professionals.

When somebody is on a mission, personal rejection no longer remains a factor. This is because these activities are no longer personal. The focus now is on serving consumers versus meeting sales quotas. The lack of passionate and proactive prospecting, selling, and influencing, unfortunately, gives way to a reactive career of either waiting for or buying leads. This waiting for things to happen, a decidedly non-influenced approach to real estate is also reflected in ads that inform the public, "I am ready when you are ready." Can anyone imagine life insurance agents (when they used to be called that) advertising, "When you are ready to buy life insurance, I am ready to sell it to you"? If this non-selling culture ever defined that industry, there would have never been skyscraper insurance buildings. These approaches are opposite to the practice of influencing and stimulating greater consumer readiness and activity. We should never forget that hard-selling leads to negative influence, while professional and consultative selling leads to positive influence, higher value, and indispensability.

Perhaps I am overly optimistic, but I believe that if the real estate industry were to devote all of its hard work, dedication to service, commitment to its clients, ongoing education, and skill development more towards building relationships than merely excelling at executing transactions, that someday we might see the following scenario occur: Instead of the media contacting real estate brokerages and agents asking for an opinion on where the market is headed, that the question might become, "Where is the real estate industry taking the market?"

My next question, now that I have asked you, "Who is the greatest salesperson you know," is, "How great a salesperson do you consider yourself?" Also, are you in a real estate career that requires selling, or are you in a sales career that involves real estate? Just as elsewhere in this book I ask that you design a pie-chart where you estimate how much of your value derives from your selling, your service, or your services—I would now like to ask you to create another pie-chart—how much of your success is due to selling, networking, or marketing/social media? I realize that you can never determine with exactitude scientific percentages and also that there is an interrelationship among the three dimensions, but there is a reason why this exercise has a lot to do with influence. For example, you can use social media to connect with people, engage with people, build your personal brand, and participate in communities. Yet, there are many people who belong to these communities who enjoy record-setting numbers of likes but do not possess the ability to sell anybody anything. So too, there are some people who are very persuasive, have great confidence, the ability to influence, but lack the range and reach that only social media platforms can provide. There are also countless real estate professionals who are prodigious face-to-face networkers and involved in numerous civic and social organizations.

Here again, though, they may not be able to sell. The reason for you to be able, to the degree possible, define your level of sales skills or persuasiveness, and thus personal influence, is because the times we are living in are compelling you to focus more on your social media range and reach versus your selling influence.

Regarding the question of—whether you are a salesperson in real estate or a real estate person who also sells. I have another question for you:

Which professional do you think makes more money on average, an average real estate professional or an average professional salesperson?

A successful real estate professional or a highly effective salesperson?

My advice is this—if your major career objective aside from serving the needs of others is to maximize your income, that means the following:

If you believe that a successful salesperson, on average, makes more money than an average agent, then you might want to consider internalizing that you are a salesperson in real estate versus a real estate person who also has to sell.

High impact salespeople have one thing in common— they all believe that if there wasn't a real estate industry, they could be just as successful selling something else. I want you to think about that. Do you share that belief? For all those who want to become salespeople in order to gain influence and help as many people as possible, please remember 'selling is a science.' Communication is vital and more important than having scripts for every situation. It is extremely important to develop deep knowledge, problem-solving solutions, and answers for each and every situation you pursue—otherwise, it is difficult to be a consultative salesperson—which leads to influence and, instead, a hard or no-salesperson that suppresses all potential influence.

Chapter 11—
Influential Marketing

Dr. Timothy Leary, a leader in the L.S.D. Movement of decades past, whose background included attending West Point and the University of California at Berkeley, was considered back then to some, as an out-of-the-box thinker, while to others, "out of his mind."

I will reference the only aspect of this psychedelic guru's legacy that would ever give me a 'high' as a way of setting the tone regarding influential marketing. Leary brilliantly stated, ***"If you want to change the way people respond to you, then you must change the way you respond to people."***

Given my scientific background, those who know me understand that I am predisposed to approaching most subjects by first looking for research pertaining to the subject at hand. In the case of influential marketing, I examined both the historical and contemporary relationship that exists between the real estate industry and the role of marketing and how this dynamic alliance impacts the manner in which consumers respond to real estate professionals.

It does not require any level of vigilant research to conclude that a vast percentage of the population does not hold the real estate industry at large in high esteem. This reality unquestionably relates to how consumers respond to present-day real estate influence or lack of same. For example, when was the last time you observed a real estate agent being portrayed in either movies or the media in a flattering fashion? Now, if you want research rather than anecdotes, a Harris poll once asked consumers (see exhibit next page) to respond and rank 23 careers by order of their relative respect. Why do you think real estate agents came in dead last, 23rd out of 23 choices?

The Harris Poll

PRESTIGE OF 23 PROFESSIONS AND OCCUPATIONS

Summary Grid

Below is a list of occupations. For each how, if at all, prestigious do you find the occupation?

Base: All adults		MORE PRESTIGE (NET)	Has a great deal of prestige	Has prestige	LESS PRESTIGE (NET)	Has not that much prestige	Not at all prestigious
Doctor	%	88	45	44	12	8	4
Military officer	%	78	34	44	22	16	6
Firefighter	%	76	32	44	24	17	6
Scientist	%	76	30	46	24	19	5
Nurse	%	70	24	46	30	23	7
Engineer	%	69	18	52	31	24	7
Police officer	%	66	21	44	34	25	10
Priest/Minister/Clergy	%	62	21	41	38	26	12
Architect	%	62	13	49	38	29	9
Athlete	%	60	23	38	40	25	15
Teacher	%	60	21	40	40	30	10
Lawyer	%	60	16	44	40	26	15
Business executive	%	58	13	45	42	30	12
Actor	%	55	20	35	45	27	18
Entertainer	%	53	18	35	47	29	19
Member of Congress	%	52	16	37	48	24	24
Farmer	%	45	14	31	55	33	22
Journalist	%	45	7	38	55	40	16
Accountant	%	40	6	34	60	43	17
Banker	%	38	5	33	62	42	19
Stockbroker	%	38	6	31	62	41	21
Union leader	%	35	7	28	65	38	27
Real estate broker/agent	%	27	4	23	73	50	24

179

How does this statistic speak to the quality of real estate industry influence?

Was it because consumers hate homes, farms, waterfront properties, townhouses, condominiums, or the lifestyles we make possible to them? "I hate homes, and I never want to see another waterfront property again!" I doubt that. Or, could it be that consumers disrespect the charismatic and convivial agent who spent weeks and months paying buyers and sellers respect—and while in their physical presence? Again, I think not. Clearly, consumers don't hate homes or those who sell them! Why then this negative influence? I address this issue in part when I discuss the reasons behind the Real Estate Loyalty Gap during my convention speeches, broadcasts, and brokerage tours. I consistently ask my audiences why they believe most consumers do not return to their last real estate agent. What is your conclusion? My answer is that there exists an unmistakable lack of positive and sustainable influence, and another contributor to this gap relates to the real estate industry's approach to marketing.

As I reveal earlier in the book, when consumers are asked whom they turn to for real estate-related advice, real estate professionals come in third. Therefore, even bridesmaid's status is not achieved! To me, this research emphatically suggests that while consumers are being profoundly influenced by real estate professionals, by virtue of the industry's population and contact volume, they are not being influenced profoundly. Why do you believe this is so? I believe the lack of profound influence versus omnipresent influence is determined foundationally and fundamentally in the way in which the real estate industry has incorporated marketing or its inadequate definition of same.

To those of you who may be wondering, Chris, what is the difference between foundational and fundamental? Here is the difference.

To me, foundational represents the way in which the real estate industry first determined and defined its value proposition. Out of the foundational emerges the fundamental. The fundamentals then become the marketing ethos that is taught for years and decades to come.

The fundamental ethos fortifies the foundation, notwithstanding whether or not the foundation is flawed.

This is why, when I attend real estate conferences, both during my years at Intero, and now as C.E.O. of HSF Affiliates, I am privately bemused when I hear speakers and coaches proclaim that the real estate industry needs to get back to the basics or fundamentals. The basics of hard work, business planning, and prospecting are unquestionably worthy of reinforcement and repetition, yet I believe there is an astonishing menu of industry practices and its overall marketing that need to go well beyond the foundational and fundamental principles.

In the same way that telling some people to "be themselves" is the worst advice you can give them, so too, categorically asserting that an industry should go back to its basics is ill-advised if the basics are now out of touch with needs and challenges.

I suggest, when it comes to inspiring a marketing meta-morphosis, that you take a moment to contemplate your personal definition of "marketing." Perhaps you privately answered that marketing means "building your brand," providing people with what they want, advertising, personal promotion, bringing a product to the market, or the word "marketing" is essentially an interchangeable synonym for selling, advertising or promotion. I believe that while all of these anticipated answers comprise important components of an overall marketing process, that when taken individually, none alone provide real estate companies, agents, teams, or for that matter, real estate brands, with a proper foundational and fundamental premise.

The best definition of marketing that I have come across, one that is both simple and comprehensive, is:
Marketing is to first determine the unmet needs of the market and then to develop goods and services to satisfy unmet needs.

Without this level of clarity surrounding the all-important subject of marketing, or another similarly concise yet complete definition, one may never leverage the true distinctiveness of influential marketing. For example, for all those who brandish their image on park benches, that is an example of potentially very valuable personal promotion and even personal branding, but this ritualistic activity falls short of the aforementioned definition of marketing. Why so? Because, ostensibly, most consumers during dinner are not lamenting a lack of real estate agents being featured on graffiti magnet park benches. Moreover, the seasonable distribution of pumpkins is personal promotion, but it is highly unlikely that consumers, upon receiving their jack-o-lanterns, will infer that such a gift is to encourage them to downsize.

When I first conceived of the I.Q. Concept, one that measures influence quotient and not intelligence quotient, it was with the idea that while pumpkins and park benches will guarantee results more favorably than the absence of superior marketing efforts, these activities will not in my view close what I have defined as the Loyalty Gap or expand one's Real Estate Ecosystem. Additionally, leading the world in the distribution of calendars, trinkets, and self-congratulatory postcards, will not help to thwart or preempt value, and fee erosion. I respectfully suggest, for the remainder of your career, before you spend an additional dollar or your precious time in engaging in what you consider to be effective marketing, social media, prospecting or advertising, that you ask yourself if these activities are truly serving the unmet needs of consumers and reflecting upon your high value.

Possessing a consumer-centric litmus test regarding how much your marketing efforts will positively or negatively influence consumers is insufficient in optimizing your marketing influence. As an influential marketer, I suggest that you also contemplate and then internalize whether or not you are truly engaged in influential marketing. In this chapter, I am devoting my attention to how you may best optimize your marketing influence directly to consumers and your clients, and not how to influence influencers. It is essential to avoid conflating terms—visibility alone does not guarantee influence. Advertising alone does not guarantee influence, personal promotion does not guarantee influence, social media alone does not guarantee influence—but influential marketing does guarantee influence. That would be marketing based upon the ways in which consumers can be influenced.

There is foundational wisdom and science regarding direct B to C, or business to consumer influential marketing. Most of you are familiar, I'm sure, with the four P's of marketing—price, product, placement, and promotion.

How deeply are you immersed with this concept is another question. This iconic premise was first introduced by the Harvard Business School in the 1950s. To this day, much of the marketing universe routinely references the interplay of these four Ps. Regrettably, the real estate industry, while accepting the importance of pricing, essentially jettisoned the other three P's. The lack of emphasis on 75% of this combined marketing message has stymied the real estate industry's overall marketing evolution. For example, the absence of a full-fledged four P approach to marketing homes led to the singular focus on why homes did not sell being attributed to price. This thinking conveniently attributed essentially all marketing failures to the pricing delusions of homesellers. This disproportional pricing-centric approach to overall marketing completely undermines real estate agent positive influence and value. If the only reason a home does not sell is due to price, then the inverse must be true. That being that the only reason a home therefore sells is based upon pricing.

This unwittingly causes the real estate industry to be asking for high-level marketing fees while pointing to the role of an appraiser as representing the source of the greatest value. Instead, if the real estate industry was foundationally constructed upon all Four Ps of Marketing, this inadequacy and weakness would not have been so prevalent. Instead, our influence and respect would be characterized by referencing the 'marketing agent' or 'marketing Realtor® versus the completely inadequate term, 'listing agent.'

Today's marketing leaders also pay homage to the acronym S.A.V.E. For them, Solution has replaced product, Access has replaced placement, value has replaced price, and Education has replaced promotion. Are words or acronyms merely the domain of speakers and authors? Might this marketing-related science also speak to you? How is the home that you are marketing going to serve as a solution? This is where influence with buyers increases, as a product does not necessarily meet a consumer's unmet need, whereas a solution does fulfill that role.

Therefore, when you are posting information, are you creating a solutions-based narrative?

Access versus Placement

Years ago, when buyers called regarding ads and asked, as an example, "Does the home have four bedrooms?" They were responded to with the question, "Do you want four bedrooms?" This was a form of denying Access to information because back then, real estate agents controlled the data. Are you consistently providing complete Access to the properties you are marketing and explaining to the homesellers how important Access is in the S.A.V.E. approach to marketing? We all know that price follows value, and in the Information Age, consumers demand Education over promotion. Accordingly, as you approach the marketing of your properties, are you prepared to include these four steps of marketing—be they either the four Ps or S.A.V.E.—if not, what scientific methodology have you created as their replacement?

Another scientific basic of marketing that has everything to do with you optimizing your influence, is to appreciate the difference between 'inside-out' and 'outside-in' marketing. Inside-out is when you base your advertising, promotion, social media, and selling based upon your needs. Outside-in marketing is when you base your value proposition on what consumers need.

In our chapter on communication, you'll read that the example is given that business cards which have a message on the back which reads, "The sincerest compliment someone can pay me is to refer me to their family and friends," would represent 'inside-out' marketing. "My greatest professional privilege would be to serve the real estate needs of your family and friends," would represent 'outside-in' marketing.

Much of marketing today, and especially books on influential marketing, owe their existence to the assumption that they are speaking to companies who have millions of dollars to spend. The focus is on how to go beyond celebrity influencers and leverage online and credible leaders—how to be more efficient with your spending and how to create compelling content based upon demographics, psycho-graphics, behavioral profiles, and a host of other predictive data touchpoints.

These teachings, including the writings of Danny Brown, co-author of *Influencer Marketing*, can be very helpful. However, there are nuances to the real estate industry which cannot be overlooked and must be added to the world of real estate influence. For example, while Danny gives us his online and contemporaneous equivalent for the power of the Four P's along with his Four M's of influencer marketing, it remains to be seen how much this knowledge will contribute to your success versus methodology specifically designed for real estate. Danny's Four Ms of Online Influencer Marketing are Make, Manage, Monitor and Measure. Broken down, it would be: You first have to make influencers through connecting with the right people. Manage the flow of content, and then Monitor what is not working, and finally, Measure results. Now, if you are wondering if monitoring and measuring might have a lot in common, this may be true, but if Danny did not have a symmetrical equivalent to the Four P's of Marketing, then he would have less influence. In other words, how could Danny compete in the space with only a three-letter acronym?

Let's examine the difference between how most corporations and brand managers seek to influence consumers and your role as an influential real estate professional—

1. You not only market a product, but you also market yourself, your brand, and the homes of clients.

2. Almost every consumer already either knows or has a relationship with two to five other real estate professionals, whereas not everyone knows five friends selling computers.

3. Many products only sell after a merchandiser has caught their attention and, oftentimes, they had never heard of a certain product or a new concept. Every consumer has heard about real estate, and lifestyle-related opportunities, therefore their decisions are less impulsive than most products or services. This in turn calls for relationship marketing.

4. Few, if any other non-real estate companies or products seeking to influence consumers work for or serve two distinct parties to the transaction. These relative peculiarities prevent conventional approaches to certain marketing and influencing campaigns. For example, a retailer is able to advertise that prices have been slashed. They can also promote that their inventory is now cheaper to buy because of a going-out-of-business sale. The real estate industry cannot stimulate, engage or influence buyers in this way, as such promotional ploys would decidedly disadvantage homeseller clients. Try adorning this real estate banner across your office window, "All home prices slashed 40% this week," and if you do, be prepared to buy personal protection armor.

5. Very few other marketers are selling identical products as their competitors.

This is why buyers do not fly into our local airport declaring that they will be calling Berkshire Hathaway HomeServices because of the brand's 'special patios' and 'distinctive kitchens.' Have you ever overheard consumers encouraging their friends to check out Real Living's exquisite landscaping or Coldwell Bankers' 'spacious family rooms?'

Additionally, programs like IDX and M.L.S. further blunt if not commoditize the consumer real estate experience. All of these distinct real estate nuances must be completely grasped when considering how to exponentially increase influence within what is essentially an increasingly commoditized industry-wide approach to rendering value.

The last area of marketing that requires greater devotion to optimizing and sustaining positive influence among consumers and clients relates to ***the professional marketing of communities.***

To this end, I salute my colleague and writing partner, Allan Dalton, for his vision in pioneering TownAdvisor.com. TownAdvisor.com did not succeed as I believe Allan's concept was ahead of its time. Allan's premise was that since people go to TripAdvisor.com for hotel information and reviews and HomeAdvisor.com for home improvement information and reviews, that consumers would welcome nuanced information, town videos, and community reviews associated with the evaluation of which city, town or neighborhood is most suitable to call home. Allan does not like it when I tell him that a part of me is happy that TownAdvisor did not succeed to the degree of his vision because if it had, he would not be my associate. Additionally, because Zillow, Realtor.com, and other real estate sites focus much more on the detailed-display of homes being marketed by Realtors® versus community-related information, there still exists the opportunity for individual Realtors® and companies to dominate this space, and fill this void before the world catches up to Allan's vision.

Why do I think that someday there will be a comparable site of enormous scale and magnitude to promote communities to the same degree as homes? It is because, according to the National Association of Realtors® research, approximately 75% of consumers are more willing to compromise on the home they purchase than the community they select. Presently, the order in priorities of consumer decision-making when it comes to purchasing is incongruent with real estate industry's marketing. This is why the real estate industry advertises, "When you are ready to buy or sell a home," and not "When you are ready to select the right city, town, neighborhood or community, give me a call."

Many real estate thought leaders profess that the real estate industry needs to do a better job of so-called 'fishing further upstream' by inserting our value proposition at the beginning of consumer search. This means "fishing upstream" to repeat that hackneyed cliché might mean starting by appealing to consumers as they pursue their community decision even before they arrive at their home selection choices.

Please remember that definition of marketing—that is: determining the unmet needs of the marketplace and then creating goods and services to satisfy those needs. If our marketing is not in union with unmet needs, what I refer to as 'one's influence quotient' will remain low. Accordingly, if consumers value which town, city, or neighborhood initially more than how they value individual property selection, this represents a major opportunity to gain exponential influence at the beginning of the real estate decision-making process. Given how real estate agents have acquired significantly greater knowledge regarding the towns and neighborhoods they showcase versus individual homes they market, this validates a possession of knowledge and influence that must go well beyond a Google, Zillow, or Realtor.com search.

Anybody willing to delve into the details that this book provides is establishing themselves as an intellectually curious and disciplined reader. I mention this because what I will write now, as it will be nuanced, is with you in mind. Let me now go deeper into 'Why' the real estate industry, to many, has never been viewed as a universe boasting an unending population of marketing gurus or savants. The lack of world-class marketing attribution is because salespeople, or someone in a selling mode, does not market. Just as somebody engaged in marketing does not sell. So too, somebody involved in selling is not in the process of networking and somebody in the process of networking is not engaged in merchandising.

For example, let's say that you went to a Nordstrom and, while having lunch, you were joined by three Nordstrom employees.

One employee had a badge that read 'Sales,' another's badge read 'Marketing,' and the last read 'Merchandising.'

If you asked the salesperson what they did, they would say, "I sell on the floor directly to customers." If you then asked, "Do you also do brochures?" The salesperson would say, "No, that would be Susan. She's in Marketing." If I said to Susan, "I love the new display with that fall wardrobe—how did you come up with that, Susan?" Susan would say, "You're asking the wrong person. You're talking about Leo in Merchandising." These distinctions are not semantical. Each of these employees possesses and has internalized a crystal clear understanding of the difference between selling, marketing, and merchandising— just as there are universities that treat each subject separately. To the contrary, for years, real estate agents were known to exclaim how they had just 'sold a home' when they had instead 'marketed it.'

Demonstrating little devotion to the distinction that when one sells a home to a buyer, they're a salesperson, and when in the act of marketing a home for a homeseller, they are a marketing person, and lastly, if two years before a homeseller sells—if an agent, as part of their real estate ecosystem—is advising people as to what their new kitchen should look like, they are a merchandising person. Because the industry, for years, conflated selling and marketing, and personal promotion with advertising, it prevented a higher level of distinctive understanding regarding the unique parenthetical properties to be found within each discipline.

Consequently, when a real estate agent is on a park bench or on a supermarket carriage and exalts these activities as 'marketing,' nevermind influential marketing, and wonder why they secure fewer listings than a colleague who engaged the community on how to appeal their property taxes or whether they should move or improve, the answer can be found in these profound distinctions. What may not occur to this 'park bench-centric' agent is that they were engaged in personal promotion, which was neither selling, marketing or merchandising.

Before I conclude this chapter, I feel compelled to point out that, historically, agents who distribute pumpkins, calendars, appear on park benches, supermarket carriages, advertise that they are 'spouses selling houses,' 'list with me and start packing,' 'discover the difference,' or 'we're the home team'—typically make much more money than those who don't do any personal promotion. My overarching point and another reason for writing this book is that none of the forementioned activities, as previously mentioned, satisfy unmet needs and therefore are not marketing strategies as much as advertising and personal promotion tactics. Allan and I respectfully challenge every person reading this book to continue seeking ways to integrate personal promotion with influential marketing because if this doesn't happen, all of the personal promotion, selling, advertising, social media, and networking in the world will not change the real estate loyalty gap, the creation of a real estate ecosystem, or truly creating clients for life.

Indeed, as Dr. Timothy Leary professed, "If you are to change how people are responding to you, then you must first change the way in which you respond to the needs of consumers." Before one constructs a social media platform or considers demographics, psychographics, and predictive data, it is imperative that one understand the present-day foundational and fundamental marketing approaches fancied throughout the real estate community as well as what makes the role and relationship between real estate professionals and consumers different in addition to where there are universal similarities.

Lastly, and let me state it one last time, it is advisable to always be clear as to whether you are engaged in prospecting, selling, networking, social networking, social marketing, social media marketing, advertising, influencer marketing, or as this chapter was expressly directed towards, 'influential marketing.'

Chapter 12—
AI and Real Estate Influence

Like many of you, when I first heard the term Artificial Intelligence, or AI, I was intrigued. My first reaction was, "Is this concept connected to the latest science fiction movie?" Only later did I learn of the relationship between so-called artificial intelligence, data, and its potential impact on the real estate industry. I also checked with both the Oxford and Webster's Dictionaries as I wondered if the words "artificial intelligence" were the appropriate definition for a phenomenon that wasn't just confined to robots and hardware but was steeped in software implications. Interestingly, among the synonyms for the word artificial were false, affected, insincere, fake, double-dealing, and pecksniffian. Undoubtedly, no real estate professional I know would care to be associated with anything described as pecksniffian. That obscure word, on its surface, at least to me, does not suggest virtue. Given this roster of unflattering meanings for the word artificial, how could anyone in real estate tremble at the thought of a potentially disruptive force, that on the surface, connotes insincerity, double-dealing, or lesser intelligence?

Even if no one else decides to join me in challenging this wide-spread name to describe this glorious combination of human and machine intelligence, my inclination is to label this phenomenon as 'advanced intelligence.' From here on, though, to avoid confusion, I will confine myself to the conventional term 'artificial intelligence.' Before I begin to make a connection between artificial intelligence and real estate influence, let's first examine the impact that AI is having upon other professions. Especially in light of a Vladimir Putin saying—that being, ***"Whoever rules Artificial Intelligence will rule the world."***

Research within the medical profession confirms that the use of algorithms and targeted software programs enable computers to outperform doctors. A notable example is the computers, which surpass the ability of doctors in the reading of chest X-rays. An entire chapter, if not book, could be devoted to the impact of AI on the medical field capturing countless examples of machines—albeit programmed by humans—outperforming highly experienced and skillful doctors. So too, the legal profession, where so much of its existence is connected to the algorithmic pursuit of precedence and established case law, are seeing the role of researchers and paralegals disrupted due to the power of superior, 'oops,' artificial intelligence. Artificial Intelligence will also become more prominent in collecting and interpreting information connected to jury selection, behavioral pattern recognition, and the leveraging of predictive data.

Stock brokerages access hundreds of millions of datapoints before making or prescribing investment decisions. The auto industry buys targeted ads on Facebook to entice potential customers based upon their documented driving distance and car preferences. Facebook, as they relentlessly assert, does not sell personal data outright. They instead sell access to the behavioral preferences and predilections of the people who populate their networks. All of these examples do not conjure anything robotic or artificial, but rather highly targeted, relevant, and timely strategies reflecting superior methods of engaging and influencing consumers based upon their interests. Now that we have properly defined the use of computers and machines, when properly instructed, as representing superior intelligence, let me move to the new version of balancing high tech and high touch.

While the real estate industry has sought to achieve the appropriate balance between high tech and high touch for decades, the impact and influence visited on the real estate industry through evolving AI poses a particular challenge. The lines between what consumers consider to be high tech or high touch are becoming increasingly blurred. We are all familiar with examples of individuals, and sadly much of our youth, who have become addicted to the social and interpersonal seduction of social networking platforms. To those unaffected, social networking merely represents high tech. To others immersed within such networks, their experiences might be better classified as high touch, where many of their human and social needs are being satisfied.

What do you think is more valued by consumers when it comes to their interpretation of whether their online experience is either high tech or high touch? I believe this is an interesting question. Ostensibly, the new version of high tech has, in most cases, surpassed the high touch capabilities of humans when it comes to accessing data, information, and in some cases, machine-powered experiential knowledge. For example, the average Realtor® might check in with their past customers once a month at best. Conversely, consumers can more easily and conveniently check-in through Google's algorithms as their spider software and Google bots search over one and a half million websites on their behalf. How much more time, on average, would it take consumers to receive the equivalent amount of information from a real estate professional than it does by their merely "touching" their keyboard.

Notwithstanding the many known and unknown implications of the AI evolution, I believe real estate professionals, if they optimize their influence, will never be disrupted due to artificial intelligence. I am convinced that consumers will continue to rely upon real estate professionals for years to come. This will be due to how our industry will embrace and employ AI as an invaluable tool. AI disruption should not be viewed as a threat. What is a threat, is the potential slippage on the value chain should real estate professionals not both elevate their real and perceived value and incorporate the many and varied benefits of AI as part of their overall modus operandi? Artificial Intelligence provided through programmed algorithms is my principal motivation behind examining the need for the real estate industry to elevate its value and influence.

Presumably, every real estate professional is well aware that the internet made the Information Age possible and has forever altered the way in which real estate information is provided or accessed by consumers. Given the real estate industry's long history of not only controlling essentially all homes-for-sale data but also making rules that prevented providing aggregated MLS data en masse and directly to the public, it is understandable why consumers are now rejoicing their newfound internet related data access. Clearly, consumers must feel emancipated now that they can enjoy exposure here within the information age to real estate data without first being encumbered by having to go through a real estate agent.

I am reminded, though, of how—like I am sure most of us—when I first enter a clothing store, I am irritated by being asked prematurely, "How may I help you?" as a precondition to perusing their inventory. Yet, at the same time, I can become even more frustrated after developing an interest in what I am shopping for when I cannot find the salesperson. This scenario speaks to what the internet has done to the real estate shopping experience. Consumers only want to engage us when they are ready, and after developing a certain level of interest and on their terms. Now that we have lost the guarantee of being the first point of contact for buyers, and increasingly homesellers, it becomes all the more imperative that when consumers arrive at deeper levels of information and knowledge, that we can outperform, or at the very least include other sources, such as AI.

Fortunately, the real estate industry rallied its forces to preempt disintermediation when the prospect of real estate professionals becoming the left-out middle person was advanced 25 years ago. Back then, I am told, that the real estate industry was warned by the then president of the National Association of Realtors® that there was a metaphorical lion coming over the hill, perhaps in the form of Microsoft, that would forever disintermediate real estate professionals. Fortunately, the National Association of Realtors®, due to great strategists like present-day

CEO Bob Goldberg, directly and indirectly, delivered a solution through the eventual creation of Realtor.com. Realtor.com aggregated home for sale data from over eight hundred local MLSs. This site also ensured that Realtors® would remain at the center of the transaction.

This preempted the possibility that real estate transactions might fall the way of eBay, E*TRADE, or Amazon. Of note is that my writing partner, Allan Dalton, the former CEO of Realtor.com, created two tag lines for the site that ensured that Realtor.com was properly understood. "Where the world shops for Real Estate online" was his proper message for consumers. For the industry, his mantra for the site was "Where property and personal promotion meet." This message spoke to the need to keep Realtors® as being indispensable and inextricably interwoven as part of consumer search.

This first wave of integrated industry-related technology reflected Web 1.0. Specifically, enabling information regarding properties and agent profiles were efficiently and transformationally accessed through Realtor.com and Zillow. To better understand the relationship between real estate influence and artificial intelligence requires possessing a basic understanding of the evolution of the web. For starters, although almost universally conflated, the internet and the web are two different entities. Although, clearly, they converge to form one unprecedented force. The internet, which preceded the web by a few decades, represents the hardware which connects networks. The web is the software that creates the presentation and sharing of information possible.

Web 1.0 describes the period in which the internet was only used by software programs as a portal for information. This was before consumers, or users, enjoyed the ability to post comments or share reviews. If the web never evolved beyond its 1.0 beginning, the need to influence consumers beyond the sharing of property information capturing the intricacies surrounding social networking would never have been required.

Web 2.0 refers to when the internet could be used, through advanced software, to facilitate interaction. This second phase of the web's evolution has been both a blessing and, to some, a curse, as so-called citizen journalism and the democratization of shared information has contributed to both exponentially higher levels of not only information but disinformation. A great example of the power behind Web 2.0 would, of course, be Facebook, who in 2004, changed social networking forever.

Web 3.0 is now being characterized as the facilitation of a higher-level use of artificial intelligence, that being machine-to-machine interaction. Artificial intelligence can also be better understood by identifying its three major evolutionary points:

Artificial intelligence 1.0. This use of artificial intelligence is when humans create rules and instructions for algorithms to follow.

Artificial intelligence 2.0. This is where machines take data and create algorithms in the pursuit of results and solutions from that data.

Artificial intelligence 3.0. Deep learning, which is where computers create the interconnection of neural networks which mimic the way in which the human brain functions to deliver solutions and recommendations without humans.

Since I am a former bio-scientist and not a computer scientist, I am not able with any precision to predict how each of these ever-evolving uses of artificial intelligence will impact the way in which consumers both prepare and execute important real estate and lifestyle decisions. What I can say with greater confidence is the following:

Web 1.0 led consumers to not require real estate professionals to learn about homes for sale. This level of web utilization caused agents to have to pay for leads at a catastrophically higher premium than their ROI would support. While most agents appear happy to pay for leads, the amount of money invested in paying for leads or referrals compared to the percentage of resulting transactions is nothing less than woeful.

Web 2.0. Facebook, social media, and the age of ratings and reviews has led to adaptive agents becoming more successful while others have fallen behind or off the real estate train.

Web 3.0. Whatever the results from machine to machine and deep learning, it will clearly require that agents develop permanently relevant relationships with consumers and particularly homeowners. While most of the industry is striving to assiduously remind consumers that they are trusted advisors, this lofty positioning will be challenged by the role and advice that artificial intelligence, and deep learning software, will produce.

Think about it. Since IBM's Watson Blue can beat the Jeopardy champions, and computers can beat grand chess masters like Gary Kasparov, how will real estate professionals hold up to the inevitable onslaught of not only data but neural network-generated deep learning levels of knowledge and wisdom surrounding real estate decision-making? Will AI's real estate chess moves be deemed by consumers to be "superior" to real estate agent recommendations? Will buyers listen to John or Susan agent when determining their integrated decision-making process? What impact will result by AI immediately and conveniently computing commuting time, likeability of neighbors, community stability, predictive trending data, home improvement ROI-related advice, probability of climate change factors or consequences, trending crime and growth of the local economy, and a wide range of heretofore difficult to access data points? In such an AI environment, will homesellers still be willing to tolerate self-congratulatory listing presentations, or instead, first turn to web-enabled deep learning generated home marketing solutions? Will homesellers instead defer to AI advice pertaining to the creation of a customized marketing campaign, one which implements a pricing and negotiating strategy based upon the negotiating history of the buyer along with all relevant demographic and psychographic data and knowledge? Clearly, the answer is that homesellers will welcome receiving this knowledge and wisdom from their agent, but if their agent does not represent a requisite level of experiential knowledge, then the agent will suffer from the 'contrast principle.'

203

As I write this chapter with its very basic and cursory examination regarding the role of artificial intelligence, I must also offer a disclaimer:

For all those who intend on only spending the next few years in the real estate business, please do not give too much further thought about the content of this chapter—

Just as I would not worry homeowners in their late nineties about the impending doom surrounding climate change-inspired sea levels. Any real estate professional counting the months to retirement should rest assured that nothing is going to substantially change due to AI in the next few years.

For those of you who have every intention of effectively managing a real estate career for years to come, I respectfully suggest that due to the increasing real estate relevance of AI, you begin to create, collaborative, as well as develop countervailing strategies in the following ways:

• Become more influential by creating your personal influencer plan.

• Close the real estate loyalty gap.

• Create a sustainable real estate ecosystem.

I cover each of these concepts within this book.

I now conclude this chapter by sharing a concept, one which Allan Dalton and I have created for our real estate networks that is designed to develop, sustain, and maximize influence with and amongst one's clients.

While I am not comfortable sharing the actual program, which we have titled as The Real Estate and Lifestyle Planning Guide for one of our brands, and The Lifestyle Planning Guide for our other brand, I am comfortable offering the concept, as I firmly believe that this idea is one which the entire industry needs to resoundingly support. Here is the "Why" behind these programs:

1. Why is it that consumers routinely settle in with choosing one lawyer, one attorney, or one financial planner yet continue to play real estate roulette when they have a real estate transactional need?

2. What percentage of consumers at some point in their life regret not owning enough real estate?

3. What percentage of consumers have developed a real estate plan for life?

4. Are agents more focused on developing their business plans than collaborating with consumers on the development of consumer/client real estate plans?

5. Who is more likely to sell their business—a top producing Realtor®, a real estate team, or doctors or lawyers who have a built-up practice?

6. What percentage of agents focus more on building a database than a client base?

The unsatisfactory answers that Allan and I came up with to all of these questions just gave greater rise to the need to link real estate agents and their clients, together and forever, through the bridge-building elements of a consumer-centric planning process.

Lastly, I cannot imagine in the near future, given the threat of both listing-side disruption and the expansion of AI as a major source of real estate relevant content, that real estate agents will remain viable at the negotiated fees they presently charge without exponentially increasing their value and influence. There can be no greater value than through the development of a client-agent relationship, one not built upon the shallowness of temporary transactions, but rather through the relational commitment of engaging consumers, and thus clients, into a lifetime of mutually arrived upon real estate planning and decision-making.

The ultimate question will be, "Will you partner with AI as a component of your true client/agent planning process" or instead will you sit by and watch as consumers and past clients increasingly gravitate to places on the web which provide higher levels of refined and customized knowledge and wisdom before you have an opportunity to take your clients there with you?

Will Artificial Intelligence Become Synonymous with Artificial Influence?

The final resulting question surrounding Artificial Intelligence is whether or not Artificial Intelligence (A.I.) also represents 'Artificial Influence.' Unless real estate influence evolves Artificial Influence will assume this opportunity.

Chapter 13—
All Influence Begins and Ends with the Brain

As a bioscience major (a science devoted to the biological aspects of living organisms), I have always had an interest in examining the complex interconnection between brain chemistry and our genes with social, psychological, and economic dynamics; and how this combination of social and biological forces relates to creating influence. As I considered the relevance of brain-engineered influence, the seminal question that I pondered was "to what degree do our brains influence us versus how we influence our brains?"

Without my brain-related scientific research, I probably would have assumed that we must merely take whatever our brains give us.

Accordingly, it would be our brains themselves that called all the shots without any possibility of brain alteration due to our decisions and behavior.

I am including a cursory examination of how the brain functions regarding creating real estate-related influence. I do so because this subject and its relationship have been largely ignored. What intrigues me is how we can actually assume that we have influence in being partners to our brain's performance. This important concept, in my view, has been profoundly overlooked throughout real estate industry-related education and coaching. I suggest that the relationship between the brain and influence should be incorporated into training systems.

When we attend our local, state, and national conventions, I am sure you will agree with me, neither the seminar topics nor the prevailing themes featured within the exhibit areas relate to brain structure, its functionality, and or the relationship to how we have the opportunity to influence our brain. To make my point, when is the last time you heard a convention conversation along these lines, *"I am going to visit the Brain Functioning booth, John. I'll catch up with you at the lead generation exhibit when I am through"?*

This lack of emphasis on "how" and "why" our brains function as they do is entirely understandable within the real estate industry. While, logically, it can be said that matters of the brain would be the presumed port of entry to all peak performance-related subject matter, such triaging of our tutelage surrounding brain functioning has heretofore not been a staple of convention seminars.

Consequently, essentially no attention is being directed towards the role our brains play as the ultimate determining lifeforce influencer behind why we do or do not do anything and everything.

The real estate industry has made either a conscious or unconscious decision to leave these brain-related matters to other professional conventions designed for Neurologists, Neuroscientists, and Psychiatrists. The closest we approach brain-related matters as an industry is the occasional forum focused on identifying personality types, or N.L.P. (neuro-linguistic programming). These disciplines, however, focus much more on the behavioral manifestations of the brain versus the role that the structure of the brain itself plays in influencing everything we do. Although each brain is unique to each person, there are basic structural similarities that allow us to draw general conclusions.

Since I am not a neurologist, behaviorist, psychiatrist, or psychologist, my treatment of the interrelationship between brain structure and peak influencer-related behavior will not even begin to approach the subject in as scientific biomedical or neurological a fashion as doctors and researchers in these respective fields would. It is my hope, notwithstanding my non-brain research-related background, that I can provide you with a lay person's perspective, although my comments are influenced by my scientific background. I trust that you will find my perspective more practical and useful regarding real estate influence than medical books or academic white papers regarding research of the brain.

As an antecedent to addressing some of the practical ways that my ongoing study of the brain has profoundly influenced my devotion to real estate influence personally, and for the real estate associates I've worked with, here are some brain-related facts and statistics that I find truly remarkable.

1. That our brains weigh, on average. about two percent of our body weight.

2. That twenty percent of our energy is consumed by the brain.

3. That our brains consume approximately twenty percent of the air we breathe.

4. That the brain is involved in twenty-five percent of our blood-flow.

5. That our brain uses thirty percent of our water.

6. That forty percent of our nutrients from our blood are used by the brain.

7. That our brain uses more energy than our largest muscles.

8. That ninety-eight percent of what we now know about the brain was learned in the past decade.

9. That eighty percent of prior brain-related beliefs have been disproved by recent scientific and technological advances.

10. That our brains are connected to one hundred thousand miles of blood vessels, one hundred billion neurons, and can perform ten quadrillion operations per second.

Many of these brain-related metrics represent brain performances, which none of us currently can significantly alter. Therefore, let's now move onto how and where we can "influence" the functioning of the brain. To accomplish this, let's visit our mythical real estate convention Brain Booth.

Were there be to a Brain Booth at our National Association of Realtors® National Convention (which I regularly attend and support), there could be no finer "booth worker" than Dr. Eric Kandel. Dr. Kandel is one of the world's foremost, if not the most revered, scientist on matters of the brain. Dr. Kandel, a Neuroscientist, Professor of Biochemistry and Biophysics at Columbia University, and Director of the Center for Neurobiology and Behavior was awarded the Nobel Prize in Physiology in 2000.

The reason why I would select Dr. Kandel, who is also the Director of the Kavli Institute for Brain Science, to be at the brain Booth has to do with his breakthrough research regarding how the brain structure "can be changed and influenced." Dr. Kandel proved that as humans learn, chemical signals actually alter the structure of the connection between cells known as synapses. This scientific discovery has profound implications in understanding both the impact of learning, not only on short- and long-term memory, as well as how the all-important structure of the brain can be altered by the acquisition of even the simplest pieces of information. We all possess the ability to reorganize our brains and thus reorganize our real estate careers and how we create and sustain real estate-related influence.

Altering the structure of the brain, therefore, for those in real estate, must take on exponentially greater importance than "Staging" a home. ***Indeed, we can actually "Stage our Brains" regarding how we influence.***

Let's examine the importance of the physical structure of the brain as it relates to its size. Volumes of research support the science that indicates there is a direct correlation between the physical size of the brain and intelligence. While there is skepticism surrounding whether or not you can actually enlarge your brain due to mental calisthenics, informational input, meditation, or physical exercise, it is universally accepted that you can increase the thickening of myelin sheaths, which, in turn, increases nerve conductivity velocity.

Researchers at Harvard, Yale, and M.I.T. (all that's missing is my alma mater Texas A&M), have documented, through the use of M.R.I. brain scans, that meditation by experienced meditators, for example, has revealed a pronounced thickness in the parts of the brain that deal with attention and the processing of sensory input. Their findings point to how the practice of meditation promotes cortical plasticity. These three university research teams also highlighted how Buddhist Insight meditation, which teaches one to focus on just experiencing stimulation rather than interpreting it, is particularly helpful to brain reshaping.

I have been meditating for years (How could I not? I live in California), and I would like to share when, how, and, what my meditation does for me, and presumably for my brain. The most vivid example of the positive impact that meditation provides the brain, and subsequently performance, is that of my mentor and the C.E.O. of HomeServices of America, Gino Blefari—who represents the greatest example of peak performance and an abundant life of anyone I've ever known in the real estate industry.

Before I leave the relationship between inherited brain size and intelligence, a few additional thoughts on this subject, I believe, are necessary.

1. Although, according to the Harvard, Yale, and M.I.T. researchers, while having a big brain is somewhat predictive of having greater intelligence than those with smaller brains, the intelligence they assert depends more on how efficiently different parts of your brain communicate with each other. This is where we can influence how our brains influence us.

2. None other than Albert Einstein possessed an average size brain. His breathtaking and incomparable brilliance and grasp on the ultra-complex therefore must be credited to his unmatched dedication to "influencing his brain" rather than its inherited relative size.

I am now going to free myself from the responsibility of staying close to brain facts that have been researched and reported and move into practical examples of how my research into the brain has monumentally impacted my career. These will be a number of general observations, none of which will be presented in either a chronological, hierarchical, or building-block fashion—just general observations that evolved from my additional brain-related research.

The first important understanding of how the brain works (that I learned years ago and focus upon to this day) is the brain's Reticular Activating System (R.A.S.). R.A.S. is a system in the front of the brain that serves as the portal by which all information enters the brain. All information is then filtered based upon the filtering instructions given to your brain based upon what is most important to you. Before my years at Intero Real Estate Services, which is one of the real estate industry's leading brokerages, I was an account executive at Oracle. Oracle is known to many as a leader in database software, relational database management systems, and for its iconic computer systems and software such as Solaris and Java (which it acquired when Oracle bought Sun Microsystems). Oracle, like Intero, is located in the world's technological epicenter, Silicon Valley. My professional years working in both technology and real estate, within this profoundly intellectual and strategic environment, significantly influenced the way in which I approached the subject of real estate influence, beginning with the importance of R.A.S.

Since the advent of the search engine Google, another Silicon Valley company, I have begun to describe the R.A.S. system as that which protects us from threats, keeps us focused only on what is important, and keeps us from sensory overload, in Google-like terms. Specifically, just as Google employs their famous Google bots to algorithmically search for only the most credible answers for the questions we ask and then rank them in order of value, so too our real estate related R.A.S. system works in a similar way but in reverse. Instead of searching and filtering information as Google does, the R.A.S. waits for info to reach it and then filters it as an informational gatekeeper, rather than as an informational retriever. While Google organizes its retrieved content algorithmically, based on either credible relevance or paid content, when considering how real estate agents seek to influence consumers, it is important to keep in mind that consumers (based upon their reticular activating system) <u>do not organize content but instead immediately eliminate any and all content that they deem irrelevant to their needs</u>.

Most in the real estate industry are familiar with the acronym WIIFM... "What's in it for me"?

Therefore, it is vital that we understand how the consumer's brain works if we are to optimize our influence upon consumers.

An illustration of the R.A.S. influence on one's brain can be found in the example that Lou Tice, a noted behaviorist from the Northwest, introduced. Lou Tice asked, "why is it that a mother can be sound asleep and not hear a car crash in front of her home or an explosion, yet if her infant in the next room merely coughs, she jumps (and hopefully the father does too)?" The explanation he gave was the Reticular Activating System. R.A.S. was indeed responsible for this amazing filtering process.

Over the last several years, I have had an opportunity to spend countless hours not only speaking and presenting to many of our industry's most productive and accomplished real estate professionals, including my Forever Agent panels, but even more significantly listening to and observing what makes them so successful. While each individual is clearly distinctive from one another and functions as essentially a C.E.O. of their business, there are also some remarkable similarities which collectively speak to their greatness. Without question, each top producer is decidedly more influential within their communities, with buyers, with sellers, consumers, and industry colleagues, than their less effective competitors. This competitive edge reflects how top producers, either intuitively or strategically, seek to influence consumers and clients based upon their R.A.S. brain function. As an example, when asked by consumers throughout their career what they do for a living, they don't respond with "I'm in real estate, but I used to be a teacher," or "I'm in real estate, but I used to work for the government for 25 years." These high-level real estate professionals also did not alert their reticular activating system when they first came into the business with the career-killing comment, "I think I am going to give real estate a try." This declaration devastatingly limits the way both they and the consumer will ever receive real estate related influence. Clearly, there is no way that one can exponentially influence consumers if they begin by insufficiently influencing their brain.

Accordingly, in light of our understanding of the brain's R.A.S. system, we are compelled to ask ourselves the following: What is the likelihood that consumers have alerted their brain to develop antibodies to conventional real estate rhetoric:

A. Realtors® bragging about themselves

B. Realtors® using the word "comps"

C. Realtors® making listing presentations

D. Realtors® all using the same words to describe all properties, i.e. "professionally landscaped" or "park-like setting."

INFLEUNCE and AFFIRMATIONS

Going back to the brain booth metaphor, while the three
letters M.L.S. and IDX would be much more the focus
of real estate conventions - if there were a Brain Booth,
the three letters R.A.S. would potentially be more likely
to positively influence your career. This is especially true
now because we are in the Information Age.

*The three letters R.A.S. may be more influential
to your career than M.L.S. or IDX.*

Accordingly, you need to protect your brain from excess
information. There are many real estate professionals
suffering from what Dr. Clifford Beard refers to as "a
malignancy of overeducation." Such awareness is necessary so that your brain can instead focus on the more
vital, interesting, and stimulating information that will
enhance your career.

This intense focus will also further stimulate nerve paths,
connectivity, and synapses. Intense informational focus
for Albert Einstein was on $E=MC^2$, while your focus need
not be that lofty. Then, instead, by gaining knowledge of
advanced market data (which enables one to elevate one's
answer to the question "How is the market?" from "It's
unbelievable" to a more informationally substantive answer) would be a recommended utilization of R.A.S.

REGARDING AFFIRMATIONS

Affirmations or simply positive thoughts cause neuro-chemical changes to the brain. Gratitude, for example, releases a surge of neurotransmitters like dopamine and creates a brightening of the brain. Researchers in numerous universities have found that by merely showing students pictures of loved ones, that their brains become instantly and significantly more active. Conversely, when they take these pictures away, the brain's activity is significantly reduced—what a great example of the power of positive thoughts.

Now just imagine if you told your brain that you love expired listings. How would that influence your behavior, and how would that influence homesellers?

1. It would alert your R.A.S. that any and all information pertaining to expired listings should be immediately ushered through your brain-gate due to its importance.

2. Imagine if you also were telling your brain the following: I can help people whose homes have not sold more than anyone else, and then they will be free to move on with their lives, and another family will enjoy the blessings of their home, plus I will make more money to provide for my loved ones. Just imagine the greater influence you would now possess. This would be a case of how affirmations working in conjunction with R.A.S. benefit both consumers and you.

Now contrast this with "I don't like to contact expireds," "Everybody else is calling them too," "I don't like being rejected," or "They don't want to be bothered." Such negative self-talk or negative influence could, unbeknownst to you, be shrinking a layer of your brain and your income. Affirmations are proven to be most effective when you write them down. You can also record them and play them back.

Another thought on affirmations I want to share is one that you may not have heard before. Research also shows that, in some cases, affirmations can be damaging. When? When people with low self-esteem are encouraged to keep repeating positive comments about themselves, do so. Oftentimes, according to studies, such affirmations actually make them feel worse. Keep this in mind if you have any tendency to try to influence home-sellers by exaggerating the beauty of their home. This advice must make sense. Unquestionably, if the slowest person on the track team keeps repeating, "No one can beat me in a race," I can see where this could be debilitating.

This is why the managers and coaches reading this book need to keep in mind that we should never be providing individuals their affirmations. Rather, in order to properly influence others, such affirmations should be self-narrated, personal, realistic, and relevant regarding their circumstances and self-esteem levels. Individuals with high self-esteem generally benefit immensely in almost all cases with affirmations.

HABITS, RITUALS, and ROUTINES
and their relationship to Influence

Before I speak to a small portion of the research I have
done regarding the development of habits, l would like to
make some observations on why I believe that habits (a
fundamental component of creating and sustaining influence) are sorely lacking in Real Estate. For example, you
don't have to show up on time. In fact, you don't even
have to show up. So whatever habit you created or had
imposed on you for much of your life, you can get rid of in
our industry.

Do your homework? Only if you want to!

Work a certain amount of hours? You decide.

You get my point.

This incomparable freedom from personal responsibility, for most of us, can be problematic, especially for all
those who place a premium on creating greater influence. By virtue of the industry providing its people with
emancipation from the consequences of accountability,
this can lead to someone who followed routines, habits, disciplines, and modes of accountability in order
to accomplish almost anything worthwhile in their life
to now experience disorientation. Additionally (and
let's call it like it is), one's real estate colleagues are not
likely to step in and discourage newcomers from exces-
sively celebrating their new freedom.

Were real estate professionals hired by most conventional corporations, there would not exist a need for them to develop important habits, routines and, rituals. Rather, such disciplines are embedded in the expectations of the job and are mandated in order to get paid.

I remember a broker in Chicago once told me that they asked one of their agents, "Why did you not show up for the office meeting," and I will never forget the answer—"I was in the middle of reading a great book."

I instantly thought, "Well, it must not have been a book on time management." Discipline and accountability, I believe, are vital in order to be properly influenced personally as well as to influence others. I learned this early on due to the discipline from playing Texas high school football.

I believe there absolutely is a correlation between developing habits and developing methods of influencing others. Where the brain comes in regarding habits is that habits become embedded into our neural pathways. Dr. Ryan Niemiec refers to this as mindless behavior. Mindless behavior should not be viewed as an unworthy attainment. In fact, psychologists consider this state of mind as representing the most lofty level of competence.

In the legendary competency pyramid, there are four levels.

Starting at the bottom, we see the lowest level of competency, ***Unconsciously Incompetent***.

This is defined as a person not only being incompetent but not knowing that they are incompetent or why. I recognize this syndrome all the time in real estate. It's where individuals who are failing or wallowing in mediocrity do not even have a clue as to the real reason why they are incompetent. Instead, their analysis is focused on excuses, i.e., "No one ever shows up at the open houses, and that's why I'm not doing well."

The next highest level, or second-lowest level, ***Consciously Incompetent.***

This where an individual or company is actually aware of their deficiencies, which skills they lack, or what behavior is missing. For this person, and the company, there is more hope.

The next highest level is ***Consciously Competent.***

This individual is in a much better position than most. That said, they must still consistently concentrate in order to execute effectively.

The final level is ***Unconsciously Competent.***

This is the category where the researchers place the highest status. This is when a person is on automatic pilot. This is like the tennis player who does not have to think about their backhand or Gino Blefari's dear friend, Dwight Clarke, who didn't have to figure out how he was going to make that iconic touchdown catch on a pass from Joe Montana.

However, attaining this level of competence requires developing habits, routines, rituals, and muscle memory. As previously mentioned, these objectives are all the more important in real estate because real estate professionals have to create their own work, while most of the world is provided work that they, in turn, process.

Habits, according to research, possess three stages:

    1. The cue (the trigger)

    2. The behavior

    3. The reward

Each of these three stages, according to brain scientists, follow the same neurological pattern. This habit-forming process, or habit loop, is controlled by the basal ganglia part of the brain. The cue is the trigger that tells your brain to go into automatic mode, the behavior is the routine, and the reward is the end of the process.

Habit changing is critical to changing behavior. In fact, much of the legendary A.A. (alcoholics anonymous) culture is predicated on changing habits, as is documented in their famous 12 steps. Without these habits, there essentially could not be influence.

Muscle memory is also part of habit-forming. Habit-forming is indispensable to being personally influenced, and being personally influenced is part of influencing others. It has been said by many that to form a habit takes approximately 21 days. I should also point out that this long-accepted formula is also subject to criticism because it doesn't take into account the variance involved in what type of habit is being formed. Regardless of the precise amount of time required to develop habits, it should be noted that the deeper that habits become embedded in the power center of the brain, which is the non-conscious compartment of the brain, the more reliable and resident they become. This is because your conscious brain only deals with short-term control; as there is not enough brainpower here to sustain habits.

Another function of the brain that carries immense importance in the pursuit of peak performance is referred to as the brain's ERN function (Error Related Negativity). This ERN brain function measures how the brain reacts to mistakes and is located in the singulate cortex section of the brain. The ERN process is a component of ERP (Event-Related Potential). Research on this function of the brain is primarily used in being able to measure, monitor, and treat those whose negative reactions to mistakes can lead to serious pathologies. When I read about this, it triggered these real estate-related thoughts—that anybody involved in coaching through the I.Q. System, or those outside of my network coaching others regarding influence, must be careful criticizing individuals for failure—this is because not every brain handles mistakes in the same way.

Of note, individuals are less likely to see as large a spike in the ERN amplitude levels when they make mistakes surrounding speed and volume than when they seek perfection and accuracy in just one objective and make a mistake in this instance.

This reminded me of two longstanding beliefs:

1. For brokers, recruiting solves almost all other mistakes the company makes. Therefore, if you are constantly recruiting and adding a significant number of new and talented people to your organization, you are less likely to feel depressed by the "mistake" of losing any one person.

2. For agents (those who only have one or two deals they are working on), when they lose those one or two deals, their devastation is much greater and psychologically damaging as regarded by their ERN than if they lost five deals out of thirty upon which they were working. This is all the more reason why I want the readers of this book to

influence a lot more consumers and clients to continue do-ing business with you—because of the psychological im-pact that success has on your brain.

This also reminds me of something I read many years ago in the New Yorker Magazine: ***"Most people think that the opposite of depression is happiness. It isn't, it is vitality."***

How does this relate to real estate and the brain? Don't let perfection unrealized bother you, as your ERN part of your brain additionally might punish you. As the saying goes, "Don't let great be the enemy of good." Instead, your brain wants you, for its health, to prospect, network, sell, make lots of mistakes, and to be influential. This realiza-tion will help you rewire your brain, enlarge the walls of your brain, and protect you from being emotionally down. If you are not in this healthy state of mind, this will pro-hibit you from optimizing the influence you have with oth-ers, both off and online.

This is why more densely populated areas, historically, struggle less with depression and mental health. It's be-cause there is too much stimulation to get depressed in some cases. I heard that in a recent year, New Jersey had the lowest suicide rate, while Montana that year had the highest suicide rate. A statistic I believe many people on the surface might have imagined being the reverse. Also, please understand that I am not underestimating for one minute the genetic, biological, and other causes for de-pression that are far more complex than my examples; yet depression clearly can be an impediment to gaining and sustaining influence.

COMPETITION and COOPERATION
and its Influence on the Brain

Now, let's examine the relationship between competition and cooperation and its impact on the brain. The research I did on this subject, albeit having more to do with psychology and sociology than neuroscience or my field of bioscience, informed my decisions on how I would lead my Real Estate networks much more than any research I've done. Before I explain why this is so, let me get a connection between competition and brain structure out of the way. Researchers from the University of Missouri assert that competition is the single greatest contributor to brain size out of three major factors. Those three factors are climate, ecological demands, and competition. Competition, however, is reported by these scientists to be the leading contributor to why our brain size has tripled since the beginning of documented time. I also found it interesting that these same researchers stated that brain sizes are larger in more populated areas, given the need to compete amongst more people. Well, if that was all the research I was interested in, I would do everything to stimulate an intense and overarching spirit of competition within myself and those professional colleagues who looked to me for leadership. Instead, I opted for a combination of cooperation and competition, and for good reason.

I remember research that revealed that when people individually compete against others, they do not perform as well as when they as a group or team compete against other groups, teams, and companies. We are all well aware of soldiers laying their lives down for their partner or team member.

Armed with this knowledge and reading that cooperation increases creativity, self-esteem, learning, sharing, conflict resolution, and productivity, I took a different approach to real estate leadership than many others. The cultures I oversee need to be both cooperative and collaborative while simultaneously fostering competition with those outside of our brands.

One of the debilitating aspects of our industry is how, at times, we can be guilty of saluting individual productivity obsessively. This practice occurs even at the expense of "demoralizing" upwards of ninety-five percent of our remaining associates. This is why Gino Blefari has made WIG's (wildly important goals) more team-oriented. The motivation was that individuals could both contribute to their own success as well as their entire office or brokerage.

Perry Buffington, writing on the difference between Competition and Cooperation, states that **competition brings out the Beast in people, while cooperation brings out the Best.**

Personally, I, as mentioned before, believe in the synthesis of the two. I want my people to be very competitive and cooperative simultaneously. I want a little of that beast, plus all the best that can be derived from cooperation.

When I first thought about writing Real Estate Influence, along with Allan Dalton, I intended to limit the content of my book to subject matter that I have researched and delivered during innumerable keynote speeches, company presentations, and writings.

Those subjects are all contained within this book:

• How influence can help agents evolve from endlessly futile attempts surrounding the acquisition of business versus retaining and growing business.

• How influence is required to close what I refer to as the Real Estate Loyalty Gap.

• How influence corresponds to the creation of a Real Estate Ecosystem.

• How influence relates to creating relevant real estate social media content and, and of course, the need for all real estate professionals to become more influential beyond the real estate transaction.

The reason why I also decided to include this chapter on how the brain influences how we all influence (even though admittedly it is a more academic and theoretical exercise, and perhaps too esoteric for some) is because— while the real estate industry has devoted considerable attention to examining how consumers can be psychologically and behaviorally profiled—I believe that a deeper look at what influences all people, and specifically how the brain functions, may be necessary if one is to understand deeper causes for both consumer and real estate professional behavior.

Lastly, if you have informed your R.A.S. system that "influence not only begins in your brain" but that "you can also influence how your brain is influenced," *you will now approach the content of this book and any subsequent execution of its teaching with the proper mindset.*

Chapter 14—
The Seven Characteristics of Influence

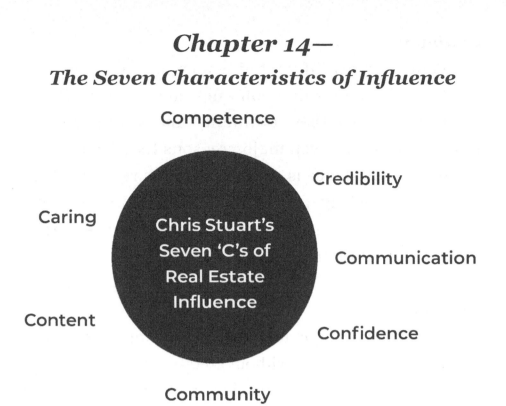

Competence

Credibility

Caring

Chris Stuart's
Seven 'C's of
Real Estate
Influence

Communication

Content

Confidence

Community

Caring

One can be competent, credible, confident, communicative, community-centric and the real estate king or queen of content—but without genuinely caring, sustaining influence is not possible.

Competence

You will never gain or sustain significant influence with clients or your communities without competence. Therefore a key to gaining and sustaining influence is to increase both your real and perceived competence. Value cannot exist without competence.

Confidence

Think of the most influential leaders or fellow real estate professionals that you know and observe. Now ask yourself, "Are they confident," and would you say that is one is the seven major reasons they have influence? Confidence is gained for many reasons—for example, knowledge, preparation, and results are all contributors. Confidence is an indispensable element of gaining and sustaining influence.

Credibility

Credibility is a synonym for trust. Also, competency does not have an opportunity without credibility. Someone who is not a doctor might be able to perform surgery, but without credibility, there is no influence.

Communication

Think of how many politicians are described as great communicators—as well as lawyers and salespeople of all sorts—while for many professionals, communication is not indispensable for success, such as engineers, pilots, or athletes to gain high levels of influence as it is in real estate. Greater influence requires compelling, consumer and client-centric off and online communication.

Content

Real estate agents, unlike doctors and other professionals, require relevant and pervasive content to achieve influence.

Community

The discipline surrounding the goal of gaining and sustaining influence must be, for real estate professionals, inextricably interwoven with the need to influence communities. The difference between serving a community and representing the real estate interest of the entire community can have a profound impact on the level of influence that is achieved by not only profoundly serving communities but also by representing the real estate interests of the entire community.

Chapter 15—
Influence and Real Estate Teams

Along with Realtor.com, Zillow, IDX, consolidation and the immense technological changes that have shaped recent real estate times—another major innovation is the emergence and flourishing of real estate teams.

How influential are real estate teams, and more importantly, how can they become more influential?

Although real estate teams have exponentially elevated the level of professionalism of tens of thousands of real estate agents—and thus the industry—I have saved this chapter for last, and it will be my shortest chapter.

This is not because of a lack of respect for teams on my part, or Allan Dalton's, nor in the relevance of real estate teams. It is because real estate teams already possess accomplished and highly influential leaders. Such influential real estate team leaders are able to dispense their knowledge and wisdom within a collaborative context to more manageable and smaller groups than within corporations at large.

The other reason why this chapter will be less comprehensive than all others is because every single idea, suggestion, and strategy surrounding how real estate professionals gain and sustain influence equally applies to real estate team and non-team members.

Moreover, this book is not intended to provide guidance on how to effectively build a real estate brokerage, real estate team, recruit and retain, perform business planning, time management, or any other real estate-related discipline other than to accomplish the following influence-related objectives—which, again, apply to real estate professionals in any and all brokerages, brands, teams, or non-teams. They are as follows:

1) Closing the real estate loyalty gap

2) Creating real estate ecosystems

3) Focusing not just on spheres of influence but also influencing spheres

4) Converting databases to 'client-bases'

5) Evolving from serving communities to also representing communities

6) Providing relevant content—off and online

7) Gaining and sustaining real estate influence

8) Building equity into a salable business

"Why then," you might ask, do I have a desire to "specifically engage real estate teams?"

I do not have a desire to speak directly to members of real estate teams. Instead, this last and briefest of chapters is directed to real estate team leaders.

This is because I believe real estate team leaders, in my opinion (with some exceptions), possess substantially higher levels of influence with the real estate agents among their teams than do brokers with their overall company-wide associates.

Is this because real estate team leaders are automatically more talented? *No.*

Is this because they are more influential than company-wide broker-owners in general? *Absolutely not.*

Is this because they care more about agents or consumers? *Some do, and some don't.*

Why then do team leaders have more influence on their team members than broker-owners, in general, have among all company associates? It's because:

1) Smaller groups and teams oftentimes find it easier to cooperate—especially when they are officially part of a declared team versus being an associate within the company at large. This special and distinct affiliation creates greater influence for the team leader.

2) Most real estate team leaders enjoy a history of successful real estate sales or are presently prodigious personal producers. They, therefore, gain influence based upon their contemporaneous credibility with their contemporaries.

3) Real estate team leaders are able to demonstrate to team members that they are the beneficiaries of both the shared resources from the overall company, as well as recipients of exclusive team-generated content and coaching within the team. This combination leads to greater real estate team leader influence.

4) Real Estate team leaders are, in my opinion, more likely to divide professional specialties, divisions and encourage distinctive geographical farms with less conflict than within larger groups. This also leads to greater influence.

5) Real estate team leaders are more able, and oftentimes most suited, to coach team members on what is required to be successful in present-day times—and in particular markets—which leads to greater influence.

While most agents, from what I can gather, better succeed by participating in a real estate team due to the more intense coaching, brainstorming, and overall camaraderie and collaboration generated by very successful and charismatic team leaders, this is not true for all teams. Therefore, innumerable agents perform better outside of real estate teams. Just as real estate brokerages do not guarantee success or results for individual agents, merely due to the adornment of the 'proverbial shingle,' so too the act of forming a team does not guarantee success for team members or their leader.

For teams to be successful, they must, by definition, provide differentiation and distinctiveness from the larger company.

The most effective team leaders are not only very honorable but recognize that (just as they wish for their team to be respected) they also should continue to respect the larger team they belong to—their overall company team and its leadership.

When this high level of mutual respect is achieved between broker-owner and team leader, it elevates the influence of each leader. Members of the real estate team appreciate that their team leader respects her or his (the broker-owner) business leader, making it only natural that they should respect their team leader. When a schism develops in which both company associates and team members sense conflict—or where non-team members are left to believe they are disadvantaged—this causes an overall, anxiety-ridden workplace.

Many top producers do not, and would not, thrive within a team.

This is either because they possess low affiliation needs or an unwillingness to be led or coached by those whom they consider to be their peers. Also, some teams, unfortunately, are formed in a way that encourages team members to remain as lifelong interns.

Worse yet, some teams exist solely to elevate the team leader in an enactment of 'Snow White and the Seven Dwarfs.'

These are the team structures that struggle for great success. Great and exceptional teams are lead and managed differently—where both the team leader and team members are expected to optimize their influence.

As an example, every great real estate team leader whom I have met has told me that their objective is to help individuals to become so successful that they form teams either within the larger team or go on to start their own team.

On the whole, I believe real estate teams represent one of the most positive developments of the past few decades regarding real estate industry evolution. The emergence of real estate teams should come as no surprise due to the consolidation of the past few decades. Specifically, when many real estate offices grew to one hundred or more agents, this made it impractical for certain agents—especially those new to their career—to receive the intense help and career oversight vigilance that often-times is only possible in smaller team-led and peer-governed groupings.

The unmistakable significance of real estate teams and groups is why Allan Dalton and I decided that it is important that I personally reach out to real estate team leaders in this chapter.

Interestingly, while I have heard many major real estate brokers proclaim that they too have a real estate team—one with two thousand members —I am not persuaded by this false equivalency. Clearly, leading a brokerage is not the same as forming and leading a team.

While broker-owners in their own right possess superior skills and business acumen, it takes a certain type of individual to work painstakingly—and on a daily basis—in the combined role of coach, trainer, manager, strategist, marketing and social media director of smaller groups comprised of real estate agents at all levels of development. Not to mention that the relatively smaller size of teams, in most cases, also compels real estate team leaders to continue being celebrity agents, which in some cases, is indispensable to both their ongoing value to the team and their allure.

Accordingly, I am convinced that no one has more influence upon any real estate agents than you—the team leader. This is the reason for my special message to you. As, arguably, you— more than anyone else—can help all those who look to you to increase their influence while simultaneously taking personal strides to elevate your influence within your communities.

I admire the clear and unmistakable, prominent role that real estate team leaders perform throughout the global real estate industry. I encourage you to take several or more of the chapters within this book and use them for the purposes of team meetings, collaboration, and cross-pollination surrounding how each member of your team—as well as your team, in general—might ***more effectively gain and sustain greater real estate influence.***

List the Ten Ways You Will Gain and Sustain Real Estate Influence:

1. _____

2. _____

3. _____

4. _____

5. _____

6. _____

7. _____

8. _____

9. _____

10. _____

Authors of
Real Estate *Influence*

Chris Stuart

Chris Stuart is the Chief Executive Officer and President of Berkshire Hathaway HomeServices, one of the world's most prestigious and fastest-growing residential real estate brokerage franchise networks.
In this capacity, he is responsible for the day-to-day franchise operations supporting more than 50,000 network real estate professionals and nearly 1,500 offices throughout the U.S., Canada, Mexico, Europe and the Middle East.

Stuart joined Berkshire Hathaway HomeServices in 2015 and assumed leadership of franchise sales within the year. In 2017, he was named senior vice president of business development and operations, and by 2018 he oversaw the daily operations of most departments throughout the entire enterprise.

Before joining Berkshire Hathaway HomeServices, Stuart served as part of the executive leadership team at Intero Real Estate Services, a Berkshire Hathaway affiliate and a wholly owned subsidiary of HomeServices of America, Inc. There Chris directed the organization's growth plan and managed its franchise company and led major corporate initiatives focused on technology strategy, leadership development, training, agent recruitment and more.

An industry thought leader Chris is frequently invited to be the keynote speaker at significant real estate events across the globe. Chris graduated from Texas A&M University with a Bachelor of Science in Chemistry and Biology.

Authors of
Real Estate *Influence*

Allan Dalton

Allan Dalton is the CEO of Real Living and the Sr VP of research and development for Berkshire Hathaway HomeServices.

Dalton is the former President of Real Estate operations for Move Inc., where he also served as CEO of Realtor.com.

Named one of the 25 most influential industry leaders by NAR, inducted into the RISMedia Real Estate Hall of Fame, and recognized as a top industry leader in the annual Swanepoel Power 200, Dalton's earlier career years include twenty years as President and co-owner of a 32 office real estate brokerage, and co-creating marketing systems for numerous real estate industry global brands.

An author of three previous books, Dalton was also a former Boston Celtic draft choice. Allan and his wife Carol live in CT—equidistant to their three daughters and nine beloved grandchildren.

Here is what Global Real Estate Leaders are saying about *Real Estate* Influence

"It has been said that England and America are separated by a common language—*Real Estate Influence* speaks our language like no other real estate book because its brilliance is so uncommon!"
Martin Bikhit, London

"The manner in which *Real Estate Influence* challenges conventional wisdom is priceless, and the recommended changes are invaluable."
Alma Cecilia Ramírez, San Miguel de Allende México

"Stuart and Dalton provide an optimistic view of the rapid changes in real estate, the importance of maintaining positive influence in the face of commission pressure and an examination, how to be consumer-centric and to be top in clients' minds before they decide to move and the critical focus on investing in current customers over prospecting for new ones."
David S. Knox, USA

"The real estate business is the industry where you are not allowed to make mistakes, so you have to be part of the best in the world, thanks for the invaluable help of being our leader."
Luis A. Mirabent, Cancun

"Mr. Stuart, your teachings are just as relevant here in Spain as in America—if not more so! Amazing read, transformational concepts."
Bruno Rabassa, Madrid

"In this fast changing real estate industry this book provides you with actionable guides, transferable skills and marketing tactics to set you up for success. A must read for Realtors-new and old-who want to be successful in this ever changing 'Age of Real Estate Influence'."
Carsten Heinrich, Berlin

"Canadian real estate professionals also need to close the Real Estate Loyalty Gap and the plan must be to increase and sustain influence ...bravo Chris and Allan."
Mark Wadden, Toronto

"*Real Estate Influence* is incredibly timely for all Dubai real estate professionals—now and from now on!"
Dounia Fadi, Dubai

"Chris and Allan, you need to bring this message to Lisbon. Influence is our missing link as well!"
Michael Vincent, Lisbon

"This book sets a new global standard for the real estate industry!"
Cesare Maggi, Milan

"*Real Estate Influence* masterfully challenges conventional wisdom and recommends changes that are invaluable to the longevity and bettering of our industry."
Sacha Brosseau, Montreal

Here is what Real Estate Network Leaders have to say about *Real Estate* Influence

"Chris and Allan are icons in the real estate industry. Their perspectives are always on point, and this book is exceptional. Real Estate Influence is a gamechanger and a must read for anyone who seeks to establish and sustain influence within their local communities and beyond. Thanks to both of you for acknowledging NAHREP and to Charlie for your important message on Fair Housing."

Gary Acosta, Co-Founder & CEO

National Association of Hispanic Real Estate Professionals (NAHREP)

"The military community has perfected the art of working within their ecosystem, this book by Stuart and Dalton shows you how to work your ecosystem to create a victory for all."

Son Nguyen, Founder, President, & Navy Veteran

Veterans Association of Real Estate Professionals (VAREP)

"As real estate professionals, we have a duty not just to our clients, but to our community. *Real Estate Influence* shares important insights into how we can expand our understanding of what it truly means to be influential."

Amy Kong, 2021 National President

Asian Real Estate Association of America (AREAA)

"*Real Estate Influence* captures the immense value of embracing and amplifying your influential knowledge in the greater Real Estate Ecosystem."

Desirée Patno, CEO

Women in the Housing & Real Estate Ecosystem (NAWRB)

Here is what Real Estate Network Leaders have to say about *Real Estate* Influence

"From storytelling to artificial intelligence, to how our brains influence real estate results, there is no better person to speak about influence than Chris Stuart. One thing I will guarantee about this book is that you will repeatedly return to it and bring your highlighter."

Tristan Ahumada, Creator and Co-Founder
Lab Coat Agents

"The book is groundbreaking for the real estate profession. Building a trusted client relationship still far outweighs our industry's growing reliance on technological wizardry. It's all about "you" and your determination to become the influencer and trusted advisor who helps to shape informed client decision making and successful outcomes."

Lydia Pope, President-Elect
National Association of Real Estate Brokers (NAREB)

"This isn't just another MasterMind guide tattered all over social media; this really is a map of the real estate ecosystem and the navigational charts you need. It resonates with common sense, morals and ethics, and speaks to the very essence of treating people like people."

Ryan A. H. Weyandt, Founder & CEO
LGBTQ+ Real Estate Alliance

"The 'Age of Real Estate Influence' will certainly become the buzz phrase for the real estate industry. Thank you Chris and Allan for your insights with this timely book."

Brenda Lee Szlachta, Women's Council of REALTORS® 2020

What leading Brokers, Agents, and Educators have to say about *Real Estate* Influence

"*Real Estate Influence* is the most relevant and timely book I have ever read about real estate. The book provides new agents with a five-year head start and will help top-producing agents to soar to unprecedented heights."
George Patsio, Boston, Massachusetts

"Real Estate Influence addresses an industry-wide need—to elevate perceived value in a way that I have never seen done before."
Tracy Kasper, NAR® Vice President of Advocacy 2019

"Without great real estate influence moving forward, moving forward will not be great for real estate."
Craig West, Indianapolis, Indiana

"Creating a robust luxury real estate ecosystem begins with understanding the laws of influence. This book is a true treasure."
Jo-ann Sloan, Luxury Marketing and Educator

"Chris and Allan have captured the essence of true disruption in the real estate industry. This is the "how to" for anyone wanting to catapult their career and become an 'influencer'. A great read for those who want to control their destiny."
Candace Adams, Connecticut

"*Real Estate Influence* is an absolute brilliant book commanding your complete and rapt attention."
Sage Hazan Blinderman & Alison Joachim, N. New Jersey

"Real estate agents and brokers are some of the most involved, connected, and caring members of any community; yet they lack influence within these same communities. At its core, the authors describe an industry where its practices are incongruent with the long-term real estate needs of the consumer, and the long-term sustainability of a real estate career. *Real Estate Influence* introduces real estate professionals to some critical thinking about our roles and offers strategies which, if followed, would result in a 'service' business as it should be - one of skills, value, and influence. In an era of influence, learning to be an influencer is key to building a business which delivers more than just a transactional experience and an astute reader will allow Chris and Allan to influence them."
Rusty Willis, Broker, Greater Atlanta Georgia Area

What leading Brokers, Agents, and Educators have to say about *Real Estate* Influence

"Chris Stuart's passion for elevating the respect afforded real rstate agents is evident throughout his book. *Real Estate Influence* not only identifies the profound need to grow influence but also how to execute it."
Derrick Parker, Dallas, Texas

"If you have ever wondered why consumers don't turn to real estate agents first when thinking of buying or selling real estate, you will find the answers and the solutions when reading this one a kind gem of a book. Every real estate agent in the world needs to read every chapter not once...but twice."
Albert Garibaldi, Danville, California

"Real estate professionals can be great at selling but without influence there is no one to sell to."
Bill Pauwels, Former Global Company President
Franklin Lakes, New Jersey

"Best real estate read ever."
Craig West, Indianapolis, Indiana

"*Real Estate Influence* is a universal concept and this book transcends networks and markets."
Julie Tran, Chairperson
AREAA, Orange County, California

"Chris and Allan have extraordinary ability to see things from a unique and practical perspective which is shared throughout this sensational book in a thoughtful, engaging and most importantly actionable manner."
Kenneth B. Baris, West Orange, New Jersey

"I'm honored to have known Chris Stuart and Allan Dalton for many years and have admired them both for their personal achievement and profound contributions to the industry. They are not only great leaders and visionaries, but have built their foundation working on the streets of the real estate business. They blend this down-to-earth, practical awareness with a perspective from the very top of the industry – and share wisdom and strategies in this book that set the stage to achieve the highest levels of success in real estate and beyond."
Dennis Walsh, Newport Beach, California

Made in the USA
Middletown, DE
28 March 2021